STEP CHA
New views on
traditional dance

Edited by
Georgina Boyes

Edited by Georgina Boyes

STEP CHANGE
New views on traditional dance

Francis
Boutle
Publishers

First published by Francis Boutle Publishers
23 Arlington Way
London EC1R 1UY
Tel/Fax: (020) 7278 4497
Email: stepchange@francisboutle.demon.co.uk
www.francisboutle.demon.co.uk

ISBN 1 903427 09 6

Printed in Great Britain by The Bath Press

Acknowledgements

Molly dancers photographs by William Palmer, reproduced by permission of Elizabeth Heydeman. Britannia Coco-Nut Dancers photograph is copyright of Homer Sykes/ Network Photographers. The illustrations from the Abbey School series are reproduced with grateful thanks to Ruth Allen and Elspeth Dunkerley. Illustrations of the Ladies' Clog Dancing Contest of 1898, Miss Nellie Martell, Miss Minnie Ray and Miss Ada Dell in Caroline Radcliffe's paper are reproduced by permission of the British Library. The illustration of Lancashire Clogs by Emile Grimshaw is reproduced with permission of David Ebbage. Photographs of Maud Karpeles are reproduced with permission of the EFDSS. Theresa Buckland's paper was originally published in the *Proceedings of the Second British-Swedish Conference on Musicology: Ethnomusicology,* edited by Ann Buckley, Karl-Olof Edström & Paul Nixon, Musikmuseets Skrifter 21, Skrifter från Musikvetenskapliga Institutionen, Göteborgs Universitet, nr. 26, 1991. The editor and publishers are grateful to the University of Göteborg for permission to reprint it in this volume. Keith Chandler's paper is reproduced by kind permission of *Musical Traditions Internet Magazine.*

For Roy Judge

Contents

List of illustrations

Contributors

Georgina Boyes is a folklorist whose major interest is in performance and theory. The author of over seventy academic articles on aspects of tradition, ranging from the significance of costume in traditional custom to performance strategies in contemporary legend and the use of colour in mock-obscene riddles, she is a member of the International Ballad Commission and the International Advisory Board of Folklore, an Associate Member of Folklore Fellows International and an Honorary Research Associate at the National Centre for English Cultural Tradition and Language, University of Sheffield.

As a writer and broadcaster, Georgina has specialised in dramatised features and documentaries on aspects of folklore. Her work has included programmes on May Day, Victorian women folklorists and popular songs for Radio Four, a musical feature on traditions of harvesting for Radio Two and *Lost Voices,* a specially commissioned series on English folk music for Radio Three's *Fairest Isle* season. She has written and presented a number of series Radio Two's specialist music strand, including *Voices from Arcadia,* on the collection of folksongs, *Voices from the Dark,* a series on mining songs, *Folk in the Footlights,* on folksongs used in theatre, film and television and *Ip Dip Doo* on children's traditions. Her writing for live performance includes *In Search of England, Season's Greetings, Harvest Home, The Turn of the Tale* and *A Garland of Carols.* Georgina's book, *The Imagined Village,* was the first full-length study of the English Folk Revival and won the 1993 Katharine Briggs Folklore Award. She is an administrator member of No Masters Co-operative, the northern-based writing, recording and publishing group.

Elaine Bradtke is an ethnomusicologist (PhD University of Maryland, Baltimore County, 1997), librarian, and occasional contributor to various traditional dance and music publications. Not content to merely observe, collect and comment, she may be seen now and then with a fiddle tucked under her chin, or a pair of dancing shoes on her feet. Lately she has been living in Japan, studying Japanese and learning about Kabuki music and dance, which is about as far away (geographically and aesthetically) as one can get from Molly dancing.

Theresa Buckland organised a series of annual conferences between 1981 and 1986 on traditional dance which provided a new focus for research and discussion in the field. Much of the innovative work in traditional dance represented in this collection was promoted through exchanges resulting from these meetings. Formerly head of the Department of Dance Studies and director of the MA programme in Dance Studies at the University of Surrey, Professor Buckland recently joined De Montford University to devote more time to research activities. Following her edited international collection, *Dance in the Field: Theory, Methods and Issues in Dance Ethnography* (Macmillan, 1999), she is currently co-editing another international collections, *Dancing Through History and Ethnography*, and completing a book, *Pathways through Dance and Culture*. Professor Buckland serves on several editorial boards, including *Dance Research and Folklore*, is on the executive board of the Congress on Research in Dance (CORD) and is honorary secretary of the International Council for Traditional Music Study Group on Ethnochoreology.

Keith Chandler has been interested in traditional music, song, custom and dance for more than three decades. During that period he has worked extensively on original sources, in particular the much under-researched local press and estate account books, while his fieldwork has included interviews with over a thousand informants. As a mature student he attended the University of Lancaster between 1976 and 1979, with history as his chosen major. He is (probably) the only man in the world to gain an undergraduate degree in the social history of morris dancing. He has produced hundreds of articles, reviews and CD sleevenotes. His subjects have ranged from sword dancing in Shetland to early recordings of traditional folk music and song on commercial 78 r.p.m. discs. But he is best known for his work on the social history of morris dancing in the south Midlands between 1660 and 1900. In 1993 the Folklore Society published his definitive two volume work on the subject, and this has recently been republished in CD ROM format from Musical Traditions (www.mustrad.org.uk).

Stephen D. Corrsin has a PhD in European history from the University of Michigan, Ann Arbor. He is the author of numerous articles, papers, and bibliographies on the history of linked styles of sword dancing in Europe and North America, as well as other topics, such as the history of the Jews in Poland. Dr Corrsin's long anticipated *Sword Dancing in Europe: A History* was published in 1997 in the 'Tradition Series' of the Folklore Society. Since its appearance, he has continued his research in the general field. His new book, due in 2001, has the working title: *Theory, Ideology, and Myth in the European Folk Dance 'Revival', 1870–1945*. It will focus on the highly ideological scholarship on 'ritual' dancing in England, Germany, and Austria, in the period up to the Second World War. Dr Corrsin has been a sword and morris dancer in New York, Ontario, and Michigan. He was a founding member of the highly innovative group, New World Sword, which was the first U.S. sword dance group using primarily European continental dance material. He was a featured speaker at both the first (Scarborough, England, 1996) and the third (Whitby, England, 2000) International Sword Dance Festivals.

Caroline Radcliffe is completing a PhD on the music hall performer Dan Leno, at Royal Holloway College, University of London. She has written various related articles and was a research assistant for the London Music Hall Database. She is a member of the clog display team, Camden Clog, coached by the Lancashire clog dancer, Pat Tracey, based at Cecil Sharp House in London. Trained as a professional musician, Caroline specialises in baroque and classical oboes and recorders, playing and recording with all the major period instrumental orchestras in Britain. Her performing has taken her all over the world and she has frequently broadcast for television and radio. She has also researched the synthesis between French baroque and traditional music, co-ordinating and performing in various programmes for the BBC and at the Wigmore Hall in London. She teaches at the Royal College of Music.

Allison Thompson is a musician, dancer and writer who
lives in Pittsburgh, Pennsylvania. She feels fortunate to have
begun her dancing career (albeit at a young age) with May
Gadd, a Sharp-trained teacher. In addition to numerous articles on historical dance, she is the author of *Lighting The Fire:*
Elsie J. Oxenham, the Abbey Girls and the English Folk Dance
Revival (Squirrel Hill Press, 1998). She has compiled a collection of excerpts from poems, plays and novels on the topic
of social dance, *Dancing Through Time: Western Social Dance in*
Literature, 1400–1918 (McFarland & Co., 1998). Currently
she is working on a murder mystery set at Cecil Sharp's
Summer School in 1912. Allison received her undergraduate
degree in History from Earlham College and her MSc in
Industrial Administration from Carnegie-Mellon University.
She records with the folk dance trio Amarallis, whose debut
album, 'Waltzing in the Trees' appeared in autumn 1999.

To the dancers ...

Until recently, we were authoritatively informed, many traditional dances had prehistoric origins. Morris, Rapper and Sword Dances, we were told – with a meaningful nudge or pinkish embarrassment – were incalculably ancient and descended from long-lost fertility rituals which involved a good deal of jumping up and down and waving pointed objects in public. These dances were extremely important heritages of the Folk. Meanwhile, lots of other very enjoyable dances, we were assured, were not at all interesting; with a dismissive sniff they were described as 'social', best done by consenting adults in private. But even they were probably far better than the dances like North Western and Border Morris or East Anglian Molly which were held to be 'degenerate'. And as for step dancing – which took place in pubs and clog dancing which had featured on the popular stage – well it was best not to mention them at all. They were not really traditional, not properly of the Folk. Then someone would ask who were the Folk ? And what was traditional ? And an argument would break out which only ended when everyone concerned decided to go off and start dancing again. Inconclusive exchanges of opinion punctuated by enjoying dancing seemed to be the way the Folk Dance Revival worked. But then things began to change ...

Intent on finding out more about existing dances or rediscovering historical traditions, researchers, mainly also dancers themselves, increasingly became involved in seeking out and interviewing older generations about the reality of performance. They combed archives for any reference to dance customs and dancers in the past. From isolated beginnings concentrating on established forms such as Morris and Sword dances in the 1950s and '60s, these studies have grown to encompass previously unregarded regional traditions such as North-Western and Border morris, the many different styles of step dance and – perhaps most challengingly – the way that the Folk Dance Revival has itself adopted and influenced traditional dance, questioning the simplistic divisions of dance performance into 'traditional' and 'revival'.

But it is not just the scope of research that has widened, the pace and volume of discovery have also grown dramatically over the past decade and produced a wealth of publications offering radical new understandings of traditional dance. If scholarship in traditional culture were viewed in the same way as advances in scientific research, we would compare this transformation to the the unravelling of DNA or the development of microchip technology. Research on English traditional dances has never been so innovative, vibrant and wide ranging.

The papers in *Step Change* demonstrate key strands in these newly emerging approaches to traditional dance. They reflect the concerns of a generation of researchers who have been prepared to challenge conventional thinking, and – more importantly – put in the work to support their changed priorities and innovations. Stephen Corrsin's and Keith Chandler's papers replace the vague generalities about traditions rooted in pagan fertility rituals with comprehensive historical documentation. Elaine Bradtke and Caroline Radcliffe extend the boundaries of scholarship into forms of dance previously dismissed as 'popular' or 'degenerate', revealing the interaction of tradition and innovation that characterises all dynamic performances. Theresa Buckland and Keith Chandler answer the question 'Who were the Folk?' with information on real lives and attitudes. And whilst the research presented by Allison Thompson and Georgina Boyes deals directly with the development of the Folk Dance Revival, the papers by Stephen Corrsin, Elaine Bradtke and Theresa Buckland all reflect the way the existence of a Folk Dance Revival has affected ideas about traditional dances.

We hope the new ideas and approaches illustrated in *Step Change* are as stimulating as the traditional dances they describe and as interesting as the people who have danced and continue to dance them.

Georgina Boyes

St Martin im Sulmtal Sword Dancers, Austria, dancing at
Whitby International Sword Dance Festival 2000.

Photo Stephen Corrsin

English sword dancing and the European context

Stephen D. Corrsin

Introduction

European traditions of linked sword dancing have proved
remarkable not only for their unusual core idea – the use of
swords, or sword surrogates, as links among the performers in
a group dance – but also because they have been widely dis-
tributed across many countries and regions of western and
central Europe for over six hundred years. References to
dances of this type in the British Isles go back over four hundred years. The international character of European linked
sword dancing is undeniable and recognised since the beginning of scholarly writing on the topic in the late nineteenth
century. In this essay, I will examine the major English and
continental 'visions' of the history of sword dancing. My goal
is to unfold a unified and comprehensive picture covering
material from the Continent as well as Britain.

The first important English writers on sword dancing were
Sir Edmund K. Chambers (1866–1954) and Cecil Sharp
(1859–1924). Sharp drew many of his interpretations of sword
dance history and significance, as well as much of the evidence he used concerning continental sword dances, from
Chambers. I will examine Sharp's use of English and continental sword dance evidence as key elements in his attempt
to develop what might be termed a 'grand unified theory' of
morris and sword dancing, mumming, and other performance customs. I will also comment on other writers of the
pre-World War II period, briefly because their contributions
were essentially variations on or elaborations of Sharp's

model. The work of the subsequent generation, educated after the World War II, will be cited as well. These later writings are of particular importance because scholars have, at last, managed to present a view of sword dancing which is, relative to earlier English-language publications, much more solidly based on both serious historical scholarship and actual performance practices.

For the European continent, I will focus on German-language research. This emphasis is appropriate because of the wealth and range of the available evidence and literature on sword dancing in German and on account of a strong mutual awareness among leading researchers and dancers in the German-speaking countries (chiefly Germany and Austria) and England in the first part of the twentieth century. In the general historiography of sword dancing it is noteworthy that a German scholar, Karl Müllenhoff, was the first to produce a series of articles aiming at a comprehensive picture of sword dancing in Europe, in 1871–76; and that a German and an Austrian scholar, Kurt Meschke and Richard Wolfram, were the first to produce book-length, scholarly monographs attempting to cover all of Europe, in 1931 and 1936–38, respectively. Scholars, teachers, and enthusiasts in other countries produced significant literatures on the topic, notably in Dutch, French, Spanish, Czech, Slovak, Italian, or Swedish, but they typically focused on their own countries and produced less comprehensive works than in German.

I begin by surveying and summarising the evidence on the history of European styles of linked sword dancing, both continental and British, from the late Middle Ages to the present day, drawing on both my 1997 book, *Sword Dancing in Europe: A History*, and subsequent research. I then turn to the literature on sword dancing, in order to examine the visions developed by both English and German-language writers, beginning with the English. In conclusion I comment on critical post-war work which has transformed the larger field: the 'invention of tradition' approach, and the demolition of the notion of 'Germanic continuity' over the millennia.

Sword dancing in Europe: a historical survey
Sword dancing was a popular and widespread style of performance in late medieval urban festivals. In this period and these communities, carrying swords was a mark of honour

and respect, and various styles of group dances and performances by young men and boys were often part of local festivities. The first records of the dances date from the end of the
fourteenth century, and then multiply in number through the
fifteenth and sixteenth. The oldest records come from the
cities and towns of Flanders and elsewhere in the Low
Countries, but the style was also well known across central
Europe and in the Iberian peninsula. The performers were
typically the young men and boys of a community, often jour-
neymen and apprentices in craft guilds, members of religious
guilds, or simply 'young citizens'. In the Low Countries and
central Europe, Shrovetide festivities provided the most common occasion, though a given community's main holiday
(such as the *omgang* in the towns of Flanders or Brabant)
could also be used. In Spain and Portugal, the festival of
Corpus Christi became an important occasion. Everywhere,
royal visits, noble weddings, and other important events were
appropriate occasions as well.

Contemporary documentation comes chiefly from town
records, showing payments, as well as permissions and prohi-
bitions. Literary references and more descriptive details
begin to appear in the mid-sixteenth century. Among these
are several poems by the *Meistersänger* (master poets) of
Nuremberg in 1560–1600, the description of Swedish dances
by Olaus Magnus from his *Historia de gentibus septentrionalibus*
(*History of the Northern Peoples*, published in 1555), and comments and descriptions from Spanish plays, among them the
works of Lope de Vega, from the end of the sixteenth and the
early seventeenth centuries.

Several contemporary pictures show the dancing in the
mid to late sixteenth century as well: a tapestry woven in
Brussels in the 1540s; 'The Fair of St. George's Day', by Pieter
Bruegel the Elder, showing a Flemish village fair c.1560; several pictures from the Nuremberg manuscript *Schembart-* or
Schönbartbücher, c.1560–1600, showing the grand Shrovetide
festivities in that city; and one of a performance in Zurich in
1578. They depict groups of dancers (five in the Brussels
tapestry, eleven to thirteen in Flanders and Zurich, up to several hundred in Nuremberg), linked by holding swords with
a hilt in their right hands and the point of the next dancer's in
their left. They are performing such figures as stepping over
the swords (Brussels, Zurich), passing under them

(Flanders), or weaving the swords together to create stable platforms on which performers could stand and present fencing displays (Nuremberg). The dancers in the pictures from Nuremberg and Zurich are accompanied by musicians (fife and drum), and costumed Shrovetide fools, well known from other contexts. The dancers wear varyingly elaborate costumes, bells at their knees in Bruegel's picture, white shirts, blackface, and garlands in Zurich, and rich and elaborate clothing in Nuremberg.

This phase of sword dance history achieved its peak of popularity in the Low Countries from the mid-fifteenth century to the 1560s, in central Europe from the late fifteenth to the early seventeenth century, and in parts of Spain and Portugal from the fifteenth to seventeenth centuries. It thereafter declined in the Low Countries and central Europe due to warfare (the Netherlands' revolt against Spain, which began in the 1560s, the Thirty Years' War in Germany, 1618–48); and the 'victory of Lent', in the 'war of Lent against Carnival', as religious and political authorities cracked down on the older, rowdier popular festivals such as Shrovetide. Other factors, such as changing fashions in popular performance styles, also played a part.

In other regions after the late sixteenth and early seventeenth centuries, however, sword dancing either continued to be found or even appeared for the first time. Records and descriptions come from the Basque provinces and other regions of Spain, and Upper Austria and certain German towns (such as Überlingen). Extended descriptions come from Flanders in the eighteenth century, even though it appears that sword dances were no longer common there. Regions in which sword dances are first known from nineteenth century accounts include north-western Italy, south-eastern France, and parts of Bohemia, Moravia, and Slovakia. Many detailed and fascinating descriptions of sword dances come from these regions in the nineteenth century, prepared by folklore collectors, local antiquarians, and writers of travel literature.

The history of English and other British dances is particularly interesting, and raises many unanswered questions. A cluster of Scottish references concerns the years 1590–1633, in Edinburgh (a royal wedding), Perth (royal visits), and Elgin (fines for dancing). For England, a pair of references concern a single Lancashire gentry family, the Blundells of Crosby, from 1638 and 1712. But significant numbers of references to and descriptions of northern English sword dances only begin in the last third of the eighteenth century. It has not been possible to prove that linked sword dancing, of any type, was commonly practiced anywhere in England until this point. The reports from the late eighteenth to the early twentieth century in northern England concern three distinct groups: sword dancing in the late eighteenth century, in various places; the styles known chiefly from Yorkshire, in the nineteenth and twentieth centuries, which came to be termed long sword; and the style from Northumberland and northern County Durham in the nineteenth and twentieth centuries, which came to be generally called by the mysterious term 'rapper'.

Several late eighteenth century reports came from Tyneside. The information agrees on a number of points: region, venue, period and occasion, music, costumes, money collecting, and related customs. Little is known of the actual dances; in some accounts linking is suggested, or a lock of swords formed. Dance accounts from York, Lincolnshire, or Cumberland, may or may not be related to those from Tyneside. Nonetheless, we have a cluster of reports which show a northern English custom of Christmas-New Year-Plough Monday sword dancing. In these reports, costumed villagers, men and boys, travel around, and perform, collecting money or 'gifts'. They might perform for distinguished audiences as well. These early reports were written by educated people, typically with local ties. They usually regard the dances as 'old', though not all say this, and in any case it is not clear what this might mean. Thus, in the late eighteenth century, sword dancing, perhaps of linked varieties, was known in parts of northern England. But it is hard to say anything more definite, with respect to the dancing's development or connections.

Beginning about 1810, a fair amount of information comes from Yorkshire, where there is a consistent pattern of development through the nineteenth and into the twentieth century. Sword dancing is now sometimes connected with the custom of plough dragging, or the 'plough stots'. The dancing is found in clusters over large parts of Yorkshire, including the Cleveland and Whitby districts in the north-east, and

other sections of the East, North, and West Ridings (for
example, the Vale of York and around Flamborough Head),
the suburbs of Sheffield providing late instances. It remains a
wintertime custom, with young men and boys using the performances to collect money. Details of the dancing itself are
limited, but some reports refer to linking during the dancing,
and to the swords being locked together and displayed as a
climax. Many reports also come from farther north,
Northumberland and northern County Durham, where at
some point in the nineteenth century the remarkable style
known as rapper developed, characterised by flexible, two-
handled sword surrogates, and fancy stepping drawn from
clogging styles. It is only from Sharp's *Sword-Dances of
Northern England* (published in 1911–13) that it is possible to
survey the situation in the early twentieth century. His and
others' research made possible both the codification of these
styles, long sword and rapper, and the teaching of them in
new regions and to new social groups. The interwar decades
also saw women's and girls' teams taking up sword dancing –
a fact which remains peculiarly troubling to certain male self-
proclaimed 'traditionalists'.

What were the key factors in the development of the
northern English styles? How did they arise? The existing
documentary and pictorial evidence, despite speculations
concerning ancient Romans, Vikings, and Saxons, indicates
that English sword dance styles are modern products. It also
appears that the two main styles, long sword and rapper, are
related. This seems probable from their closeness both in
time and location. There are general stylistic similarities as
well, such as the use of the circle as the base figure in all
known Yorkshire long sword and Tyneside rapper dances, and
the small number of dancers (typically six or eight in long
sword, and five in rapper). Moreover, the customs which
frame both styles – the winter season, the accompanying
characters, the songs – are consistent, and connect both long
sword and rapper to the late eighteenth-century reports as
well. Many questions remain, however. For example, the
available information does nothing to connect the 1638 and
1712 Lancashire dances (the Blundell family reports) with
later ones, or the well known Revesby, Lincolnshire, performance of October, 1779, presented on the property of the
great naturalist and President of the Royal Society, Sir Joseph

Banks. The same is true for the limited evidence from Cumberland.

To take the story further afield, the evidence from Perth and other Scottish cities from 1590–1633 is quite different from English material. The well known dance from Papa Stour, Shetland, first described in the 1820s, is even more remote from England in geographical terms; moreover, it has a number of features distinguishing it from English styles. While the Papa Stour dance has been modified to resemble Yorkshire long sword styles more closely, that appears to be a recent development, dating perhaps to the 1920s–50s.

Some intriguing possibilities concern the idea of connections between British (both English and Scottish) and continental dances. The issue has received some attention; Sharp included considerable continental supporting material in the introductions to his *Sword-Dances*, and later writers including Rolf Gardiner and Violet Alford tried to develop explanatory models covering Britain as well as the Continent. It is possible that linked sword dancing developed in Britain without outside influence. But it cannot be ruled out that one or more of the early cases of sword dancing in Britain, or of the distinctive English styles, was the result of contact with dancing on the European Continent. Britain was not culturally isolated. The Low Countries lay just across the North Sea, and England's and Scotland's contacts with northern Germany and Scandinavia were extensive.

English performers and musicians were popular in central and northern Europe in the sixteenth and seventeenth centuries, and Scottish merchants and traders were to be found in many cities of the same regions. Could English players, or Scottish traders, or indeed soldiers or travellers of either nation, have seen linked sword dance in the Low Countries, or Germany, or Sweden, and taught versions at home which eventually caught on? It is an appealing idea, but the timing is a problem: in these lands, sword dancing was past its heyday well before the style caught on in north-eastern England, in the late eighteenth century. However, perhaps it is true for the early dances in Scottish cities. Another possibility is that a style was brought by immigrants, again perhaps from the Low Countries or central Europe. It is also the case that linked sword dancing was well known in northern Spain at the same time that it was catching on in northern England, though the Spanish (or Basque and Galician) styles were quite different from anything that developed in England. It is possible that documentary evidence awaits in some obscure archive or library to prove connections, or for that matter independent invention. Yet there is no need for a single 'correct answer' to the questions concerning the development of English sword dance styles. It remains possible that, in England as in Scotland, there were several separate 'inventions' or 'borrowings'.

English visions
The first attempts by English writers to pull together substantial evidence and create coherent pictures of the development and significance of sword dances were E.K. Chambers' *The Mediaeval Stage*, published in 1903, and Cecil Sharp's 'primarily practical' manual, the three thin volumes of his *Sword-Dances of Northern England*, published in 1911–13. Examination of the conceptual introductions to Sharp's volumes shows that he draws heavily on Chambers. This is apparent both from the speculations on sword dance history and significance which Sharp presents, and from the sources he cites, both British and continental. It is noteworthy that while Sharp footnotes Chambers on a couple of specific pieces of evidence, he does not acknowledge his larger debt in his book. Nor does Sharp directly refer to Sir James Frazer's *Golden Bough* in his introductions, though the latter's influence is also obvious, perhaps mediated through Chambers.

A major theme in Chambers' book is the importance of pagan folk rituals in the development of medieval European drama, that is, 'the *ludi* of the village feasts, bearing witness, not only to their origin in heathen ritual, but also, by their constant tendency to break out into primitive forms of drama, to the deep-rooted mimetic instinct of the folk.'[1] Chambers clearly finds these rituals appealing, but also recognises that they, 'contributed but the tiniest rill to the mighty stream' of modern drama, particularly as compared to the Christian church and its holidays and liturgies.[2] Robert Ackerman in his *The Myth and Ritual School: J.G. Frazer and the Cambridge Ritualists* elaborates on Chambers' reliance on Frazer's *Golden Bough*: 'Chambers ... found in *The Golden Bough* and its author exactly what he wanted at exactly the right moment.' (Chambers began writing in 1895; therefore *The*

Golden Bough for him was the two volume first edition of 1890, which gave more importance to ritual origins than did its two successors.) Frazer was an anticlerical rationalist like Chambers, and there must have been an instant meeting of the minds; the result is that *The Mediaeval Stage* is packed with references to *The Golden Bough*.[3]

The notion of the significance of primitive rituals in the history of dance and drama seems to have been much in the air in educated circles in England. For example, Sharp cites the work of the leading scholars among the 'Cambridge Ritualists', Jane Harrison and Gilbert Murray. That group of classicists finds the origins of classical drama in ancient Greek religious rituals. Chambers similarly sees purported folk rituals playing a significant role in the development of medieval drama. This approach inclines to trace 'survivals' of these rituals, whether in the field of classical Greek drama, European drama in general, or (like Sharp) in contemporary English folk performance. Sharp draws heavily on Chambers for documentary evidence, making very significant but highly selective use of continental European sword dance materials in the theoretical introductions to his *Sword-Dances*. He cites the articles of German scholar Karl Müllenhoff; an English translation of an account of the French sword dance, the 'Bacchu-Ber', from the journal *Folk-Lore*; and an article by R.M. Dawkins on Thracian mumming.

What is the particular significance of sword dance material in Sharp's attempt to develop a picture of morris dancing and other possibly related performance customs and practices? Sword dance, for Sharp, is a critical element in his attempt to create what might be termed a 'grand unified theory' of morris. First of all, to him all these practices were 'morris', all grist for the mill: Cotswold morris dancing, mumming and mummers' plays, sword dancing, and the Abbots Bromley horn dance. He notes the common and variable usage of the term 'morris' across a broad range of English performance customs as justification for this notion: 'the sword-dancer of Northern England, the Morris-dancer of the Midlands and the South, and the mummer of all England and Scotland, are in the popular view as one, and pass under the same name. This is at least a significant point: a common name suggests other points of community – perhaps community of origin.'[4]

Sword dancing provides Sharp with a wealth of additional evidence, and serves to expand his temporal and geographical range back to the late Middle Ages and across much of the European Continent. He uses the continental sword dance material (there was, in Sharp's day, little ready evidence on continental 'morris') to support and extend his picture, which is nonetheless primarily based on English evidence. Sword dancing could also be linked to mumming, through the existence of a few longer and more elaborate plays associated with sword dances, particularly (for Sharp) the Ampleforth dance, and through the stereotypical combat using mock swords in many mummers' plays. It is noteworthy that certain types of 'morris', however, remain essentially outside Sharp's vision, or at least on the far margins. These types are north-west morris styles, which are urban, loud, and relatively open to female participation; and 'border' morris and 'molly', which seem low and degenerate. The ideal for Sharp is presented by Cotswold or south Midlands morris: male dancers dressed in white, performing on the greens of picturesque, southern English villages.

Cotswold morris, however, does not provide much material that can be readily interpreted as ritualistic or pagan survivals, though Sharp tries to interpret it that way, as in the following passage: 'In the Whit-hunt at Field Town, the Lamb Ale at Kirtlngton, the ox-horns, chalice and sword at Abingdon, it is easy to discern traces of the animal sacrifice and the sacramental feast that followed it.' The Abbots Bromley horn dance, a peculiar and unique performance which had the advantage of superficial mysteriousness, is worked in as a 'survival' of hunting customs and sacrifices of sacred animals.[5] Sword dancing presents, by contrast, seemingly wonderfully useful evidence for Sharp's (and Chambers') notions of sacrificial survivals. It must have seemed exciting confirmation of an exotic model to Sharp and his contemporaries and successors. Sword dancing makes use of actual weapons, or their surrogates, and many of the historical records and present customs included acts that could be seen as mock 'killings' followed by ritual 'resurrections'. As for the seemingly insurmountable distinction in implements – swords as opposed to the sticks or handkerchiefs of Cotswold morris – it is simply declared that the latter had been substituted for the former at some undefined time.[6]

In the introduction to his third *Sword-Dance* volume, Sharp recapitulates the key elements of his model: 'two conclusions concerning the origin and meaning of the sword dance were arrived at: 1) That the dance originally formed part of a ceremony quasi-religious or magical in character, the purport of which was to promote the fertility of the soil and of all living things; 2) That the central ritual act was the killing and subsequent restoration to life of a man who, from the character of his dress and other considerations, represented, apparently, the animal world.' This was also linked to rites for the turn of the year: 'The resulting rite was based upon the principle of mimetic magic, the conception that like produced like and that a desired effect could be attained by imitating it. In this particular case, therefore, the magic rite took the form of a mock death followed by a mock resurrection, in imitation of the cyclic death of the Old Year and the rebirth of the New.'[7]

Sharp adapts this model from Chambers, who had just written that the morris dance was 'really identical' with sword dancing.[8] Chambers sees this identity as resting on a number of associations: the use of the term 'morrice' for the Revesby sword dance and play, the alleged identity of sticks with swords, and – a point taken from Frazer, who took it from German scholar Wilhelm Mannhardt – the use of bells in some continental sword dances. Chambers refers to sword dancing as 'agricultural', and maintains that, 'the use of swords in the dance was not martial at all; their object was to suggest not a fight, but a mock or symbolical sacrifice'.[9] Further, he states that, 'The festival customs include a number of dramatic rites which appear to have been originally symbolical expressions of the facts of seasonal recurrence lying at the root of the festivals themselves.'[10]

Sharp makes extensive use of a now forgotten article which appeared in 1906 in the *Journal of Hellenic Studies*, and which deserves more attention: R.M. Dawkins, 'The Modern Carnival in Thrace and the Cult of Dionysus'.[11] With its continental material, and emphasis on survivals from classical antiquity, it aids Sharp considerably in his attempt to built a pan-European, unified theory, reaching back into the ancient Mediterranean world. Dawkins draws on an 1897 article by G.M. Vizyenos, and Dawkins' own observations of Carnival

(Shrovetide) festivities in the village of Haghios Gheorghios (St George) in Thrace.

Dawkins begins by emphasising the archaeology of the region and the monuments which survive from classical antiquity; this sets a 'survivals' mood for the essay. In the actual performance, there are many familiar elements, reminiscent of Shrovetide festivities elsewhere in Europe: masking and animal guising, crude costumes with bells, stereotypical characters (including Gypsy smiths with a plough), groups travelling about a village performing for money or engaging in a kind of ritualised thievery, phallic symbols and obscene horseplay (which could always be interpreted as fertility-related), and a mock marriage and a mock killing. Dawkins refers to similar carnival customs from other Greek villages, and cites Frazer and the possible survivals of Dionysian rituals:

> These observances fall into line with the numerous spring festivals of the spirit of vegetation, of which Dr. Frazer has written at length in the *Golden Bough* ... But such a custom in Thrace suggests also a survival of the worship of Dionysus, upon which recent researches have thrown so much light. The circumstances are favourable to such a survival in a Greek community occupying the old city of the kings of Thrace, and surrounded and isolated by later elements of the population, Bulgarian and Circassian.[12]

One point that Sharp seizes upon as especially significant is the mock killing of one of the performers. Dawkins writes: 'After the lamentation ... the dead man suddenly came alive again and got up, thus ending this part of the play.'[13] Sharp interprets this as an act of ritual revival, such as could be found in some English mummers' plays. But Dawkins only refers to the man coming alive, without further explanation.

Sharp uses Dawkins in a curious way to link Abbots Bromley with morris in general. A character with a bow appears both in Dawkins' play, and the Abbots Bromley dance; to Sharp, the bow is an 'instrument of sacrifice', akin to the sword, though in fact the bow is not used for that in the English dance. (In Dawkins' play, it is used in a mock killing.) Sharp also states that English mummers and morris dancers, Dawkins' Thracian mummers, and the Abbots Bromley horn dancers all typically are accompanied by 'Fool, Woman and Hobby Horse'. Further, some of the Thracian mummers 'wear hairy caps', which in Sharp's view seems to be an element of animal guising, thus akin to the horn dance.[14] In identifying these points of alleged identity between English and Thracian mumming customs, he presents Dawkins' research as uncovering an ancient, enduring pan-European tradition, still extant in fragmentary form from England to Greece, and surviving or deriving from pagan sacrificial rituals. From a more scholarly and historically-informed point of view, of course, this makes no sense; these are mere fragments with superficial similarities that mean very little taken out of context.

The introductions to his *Sword-Dances* are tied together with reference to Gilbert Murray, a leading classicist and 'Cambridge ritualist', by quoting a summary of Murray's views of the ritual structure of Greek tragedy from his intellectual ally, Jane Harrison's book, *Themis*. Sharp states Murray's view that, 'Greek Tragedy is in origin a Ritual Dance'. Certain elements appear consistently, including a 'ritual or sacrificial death' of the 'Year-Daimon' with a subsequent 'Resurrection or Apotheosis'. Sharp maintains that, 'Incredible as it may seem, we have, then, in the folk-play, of which our Ampleforth dance is an example, the ritual-form upon which, as upon a warp, was woven the rich fabric of Attic drama.'[15]

Sharp and his successors created a remarkable standard vision, which, while ignored by scholars, has had enormous influence on the popular image of the English folk dance and music 'revival'. In retrospect, and in the light of recent historical research, it seems a very peculiar vision indeed. Yet Sharp cites some of the leading scholars of his day – Frazer, Chambers, Harrison, and Murray – and in his belief in the survival of ancient sacrificial rituals in English folk customs, he is pursuing widely (if not universally) accepted themes in the scholarly literature of the time.

It may seem unfair to subject Sharp's conceptual introductions to too much close scrutiny. He was not a professional scholar, and his writings bear all the marks of the amateur: highly selective and superficial, as he followed what might be termed a 'magpie' approach, picking out and rearranging cer-

tain glittering bits but ignoring or unable to see larger patterns or contexts. (Yet this approach is very reminiscent of
Frazer's method, and Frazer's scholarly credentials are
beyond reproach.) One must recall that Sharp's aims were not
scholarly; his interests were 'primarily practical', in his
attempt to generate enthusiasm for English folk dances,
songs, and music. Sharp proved so influential that his writings must be examined and analysed; but attempting to
impose consistency on Sharp's peculiar views and scattershot
methods can only lead to considerable frustration on the part
of the scholar.

Sharp published his *Sword-Dances* as he was building up
the new English Folk Dance Society, and establishing its near
monopoly position in the field of promoting the teaching of
folk dancing and music in England – the so-called 'revival'.
In the 1920s–30s, after Sharp's death in 1924, several writers
with close ties to the Society (subsequently renamed the
English Folk Dance and Song Society) wrote about the development and significance of sword dancing both in England
and on the Continent. They remained almost completely
within the 'ancient ritual survival' framework established by
Sharp, though they elaborated on some points and introduced additional evidence.

In the interwar years Violet Alford's important contribu-
tion consisted of articles and books concerning dance in
Spain and France. Her, 'Travels in Search of Dance and
Drama' (to paraphrase the title of her 1956 memoirs) remain
most interesting for the immediacy of her observations. Rolf
Gardiner, one of the most controversial personalities in the
English folk 'revival', promoted a vision of northern
European, indeed 'nordic', cultural and historical unity, in
which the rituals of sword dancing allegedly common to
Germany, England, and Scandinavia play significant roles.
Joseph Needham, in later years one of the greatest names in
sinology, in the 1930s attempted to produce a classified index
of English ritual dance references, which could serve as the
basis for scholarly research. But none of these writers did
much to further *scholarship* in the field: Alford's writings
remain interesting as 'travels in search of literature',
Gardiner's as political curiosities, and Needham's as merely
a first step which no one pursued till E.C. Cawte and his col-
laborators, c.1960, published a larger classified index.[16]

Despite the obvious weaknesses of Sharp's 'ancient ritual survival' model it was not challenged in the interwar decades. In fact, one of the more interesting attempts to contribute to the interwar 'English vision' was made in the 1930s by an Austrian scholar, Richard Wolfram, as we shall see later.

German and Austrian visions

German-language scholarship and writing on the topic of sword dancing has been considerably more substantial, wide ranging, and scholarly than that in other languages, including, until the 1990s, work in English. German and Austrian academics and enthusiasts have also looked to the essential picture of sword dancing as an ancient ritual survival. However, they differ from the English writers, focusing on what they regarded as ancient German elements, and on the idea of sword dances as deriving from rituals of men's secret societies and rituals (the idea of the *Männerbund*). The theme of an alleged 'continuity' (*Kontinuität*) in German culture, over thousands of years, has had particular significance.

The first author to assemble and describe a significant part of the wealth of evidence was Karl Müllenhoff, a professor in Berlin who published three articles on sword dancing in the 1870s. His articles are most useful for the extensive material that he gathered. Müllenhoff, a classicist as well as Germanist, frames the discussion for German-language scholars of several subsequent generations.[17] He draws on many fields, bringing in not merely late medieval and early modern German historical material but also that from other countries. Nonetheless, it is his use of a passage from the *Germania*, the Roman author Tacitus' small book on the German tribes, written in the late first century AD, that has proved most significant. Müllenhoff attempts to establish a direct connection between Tacitus' account of ancient German dancing, and the late medieval and early modern styles of linked sword dancing. Tacitus comments in chapter 24 of the *Germania*:

> Their public spectacles boast of no variety. They have but one sort, and that they repeat at all their meetings. A band of young men make it their pastime to dance entirely naked amidst pointed swords and javelins. By constant exercise, this

kind of exhibition has become an art, and art
has taught them to perform with grace and
elegance. Their talents, however, are not let out
for hire. Although some danger attends the
practice, the pleasure of the spectator is their only
recompense.[18]

There is no evidence which can reasonably connect or
identify Tacitus' account of ancient Germans warlike performance with dances that begin to appear in the historical
record only thirteen hundred years later in many different
European countries. So why has this supposed connection
appealed so much to German-language writers? Tacitus'
works were rediscovered by European scholars in the fifteenth century. Despite the fact that the *Germania* was a dis-
tinctly minor work among Tacitus' surviving oeuvre, it
proved of critical importance in the development of German-
language nationalistic writings; in part because it seemed to
provide such useful ancient evidence on the Germans by a
classical Roman writer, and in part because it could be used
to present the Germans as particularly noble in a savage way
(though to do this, one must ignore the negative comments
which Tacitus also made). The *Germania* served, up to the
Second World War, as a primary source – even a 'Bible' – for
German-language ethnocentric writing.[19]

It also became a key source for German-language writing
on sword dance. The identification of Tacitus' dance with
contemporary German ones was first made in 1551, when the
scholar Jodocus Willich wrote a commentary on the
Germania, in which he says that this dance of the ancient
Germans is now known as a sword dance (*eyn schuuerdtanz*, or
chorea gladiatoria). In the seventeenth and eighteenth centuries, references to the Germania appeared in writings about
sword dancing not only in German-speaking lands, but also
in England, the Low Countries, and even Spain.

This brief passage in the *Germania* has been used over and
over again to justify the view that late medieval and modern
styles of linked sword dances, which are found in many lands
and among many peoples, derive from ancient German tribal
rites. Again, there is no evidence to support this notion, and
no way to bridge the gap between Tacitus and the late
medieval and modern reports. Tacitus' remarks appealed to
scholars for two reasons. First, nationalistically minded writ-

ers in Germany and Austria have found in them grounds for
an ancient German origin for sword dancing. Second, seekers
of prehistoric roots have claimed that this isolated passage is
proof that the style goes back at least two thousand years,
instead of the six centuries of late medieval and modern
records. It thus draws both on ethnic chauvinism and nationalism, and on the same 'doctrine of survivals' which produced
the view of sword dances as survivals of ancient rituals in
England.

Tacitus actually seems to have written his *Germania* as an
indirect attack on what he saw as the degenerate oversophis-
tication of imperial Rome, contrasting it with the noble sav-
agery of the German tribes, and as an exercise derived from a
style of literary ethnography that went back to earlier Greek
models. (Many phrases appear to have been lifted from Greek
writings on other barbarian peoples.) It can hardly be regarded as a factual document in an evidentiary sense. This was
recognised in the interwar years by a few scholars, but any
critical approach was received as an attack on the reliability
of Tacitus, and thus on the ancient German heritage, and on
German national feeling in general.

In the decades after Müllenhoff's studies, a number of
publications by philologists, historians, and folklorists in
Germany, Switzerland, and the Austro-Hungarian Empire
followed. Scholars and antiquarians combed local archives
and historical chronicles, tracking down materials on performances from all across central Europe. They concentrated on
German-speaking communities, rarely showing interest in
evidence from other lands. Some also discussed existing
dances, where these could be found in Germany and in several provinces of Austria-Hungary. They produced new evidence, but little in the way of new ideas distinct from
Müllenhoff's.

One of the more interesting figures in the German literature of sword dancing was the Germanist Hans Naumann. He
was a well known literature scholar and sometime folklore
specialist. He was something of a scholarly celebrity, and
taught as a visiting professor in North America as well as lec-
turing in many German and European cities. He also was one
of the most controversial figures in interwar German folklore
scholarship. He relied on the idea of folklore as 'sunken cultural values' (*gesunkene Kulturgüter*). Essentially, this is the

idea that the mass of humanity is completely uncreative;
instead, folklore (songs, dances, etc.) consists of cultural elements that 'sink' from the creative upper classes. It is a concept that had a superficial, simple appeal but could not stand
up to scholarly scrutiny. It led to a lively discourse in the
interwar years among scholars in the German-speaking
countries.[20]

Naumann made significant use of sword dance plays in his
two most important monographs, published in 1921–22,
though he shows little interest in the dances as such. One of
his students, Paul Jacques Bloch, published a few years later
a doctoral thesis which attempts to apply Naumann's con-
cepts systematically to folk dances – which Bloch divides (as
many have) into ritual dances and social dances. Bloch and
Naumann both were sharply attacked in the early 1930s by
Richard Wolfram, then just starting out on his career as a
folklorist.[21] Naumann, though he became a Nazi party member in 1933 and made sycophantic speeches on such occasions
as Hitler's birthday, was attacked by other Nazis as a 'liberal',
because his theory emphasised class differences rather than
the unity of the nation and race. Also, a leading French
anthropologist of Jewish origin, Lucien Lévy-Brühl, was an
important source for some of Naumann's views. Naumann
left little in the way of a legacy to the field of sword dance
research but his works still make interesting, if superficial
reading. He was also a fascinating case study in scholarly
sycophancy in the Nazi era.

The first book-length, scholarly monograph on sword
dancing drew on Naumann for, at least, intellectual inspiration. This was Kurt Meschke's *Schwerttanz und
Schwerttanzspiel im germanischen Kulturkreis* (*Sword Dance and
Sword Dance Plays in the Germanic Cultural World*, 1931). It is
an awkward work, in that it reads like the academic disserta-
tion it was, but it pulls together a great deal of historical
material. Meschke attempts to tie his work to larger historical
themes: for example, he draws on Müllenhoff's advocacy of
the connection to Tacitus, and tries to fit it into the historical
context of the German *Völkerwanderung*, the 'wandering of
peoples' in the late Roman and early medieval periods. The
book's strength is its wealth of historical detail; its weakness
is the speculative, unsupportable structures linking sword
dancing to very unlikely ancient German historical and cul-

tural developments.

Meschke cannot be accused of being an extreme German nationalist; in fact, he and his family fled Germany for Sweden on the eve of the Second World War. Yet his work illustrates the pervasive nature of German nationalism in the literature on sword dance. That is, he falls prey to ethnocentrism in scholarly guise when he claims not only that the style was widespread in German-speaking regions – a fair statement – but that it was also more broadly 'Germanic' in essence and spirit. It also illustrates the slippery nature of the term 'Germanic' (which is a legitimate term in linguistics, but not medieval or modern history), by using chiefly German and Austrian material, and selected Scandinavian and British evidence, but mostly ignoring the rich evidence from the Low Countries. The proper term translated as 'German' in English is, of course, *deutsch*, while *germanisch* is translated as 'Germanic' and refers properly to the language family, but loosely to the countries, peoples, and cultures of most of northern and central Europe, from antiquity to modern times.[22]

By far the most significant name in interwar German-language scholarship on sword dancing is that of Richard Wolfram (1901–95). Wolfram's professional achievements, primarily as a professor at the University of Vienna but also in other areas of *Volkskunde*, are very impressive; perhaps the most impressive single point, to academics, would be his supervision of approximately forty-five doctoral dissertations in his career. Yet these achievements are overshadowed by his deep involvement in National Socialism. He was a party member in Austria from 1932, showing he was not merely an opportunist such as those who joined up after the 1938 Anschluss; he was a leading figure in the Nazification of his university and of Austrian scholarship in general in 1938–45; and he ranked high in the *Ahnenerbe* (ancestral heritage), the intellectual department of the Nazi SS. After the war, despite being deprived of his professional positions for some years, he seems never to have repudiated or apologised for any of his actions or statements in the Nazi years. He published the results of his Nazi-era research without apology or explanation. He was both a committed Nazi, and an opportunist who took great personal and professional advantage of terrible events.

Wolfram began his academic career as one of a group of young scholars around the Vienna classicist and folklorist Rudolf Much (1862–1936). This group became known as the 'Vienna Ritualists', so-called because of their general contention, in the debate over whether myths preceded or derived from ritual activities in primitive societies, that the latter was true – that is, that ritual activities preceded mythologies. Other members of this group included most notably Otto Höfler, Wolfram's closest intellectual ally and like him a committed (and professionally successful) Viennese Nazi, and Lily Weiser-Aall. Höfler and Weiser promoted the idea of the importance of secret male groups – *Männerbünde* – in German culture. Höfler in particular maintained that these groups were not only important in antiquity, but survived into the modern era, and that they were of the greatest significance in the development of the German state idea. Höfler's ideas were most useful to the SS, which saw itself as a continuation of such secret *Männerbünde*.[23]

Wolfram draws the idea of *Männerbünde* from Weiser and Höfler, maintaining that sword dances were in essence the initiation rituals of such groups. He places great emphasis on what he perceives to be the profound ritual significance of sword dances. He ties the dances to men's societies and groups, secret or open, and to their initiation rites for young men: 'He who wishes to understand sword dancing must understand the world of groups in all its variety.'[24] To support his views, he uses not only much of the same historical material as Meschke had compiled (if with less facility in historical analysis than Meschke displayed), but also draws upon random ethnological and anthropological supporting evidence from throughout the world – the same sort of 'magpie', context-free approach that Frazer and Sharp had used. Wolfram's main work is his *Schwerttanz und Männerbünde* (*Sword Dancing and Male Groups*). The first half appeared in three parts in 1936–38, but Wolfram never published a complete edition. Wolfram is a fluent writer but shows little facility in historical analysis or in discussing processes of change over time. He is also overly concerned with proving a German origin or even racial character for sword dancing. Wolfram knew English well and spoke at meetings of the EFDSS in both 1932 and 1935. The papers printed in the Society's *Journal* provide handy summaries of his ideas to non-German readers.[25] Wolfram's views have dominated German-language research since the 1930s. In the years since the Second World War, despite advances in research in Germany and Austria as elsewhere, there have been no comprehensive attempts to rethink the models and approaches based on his (and Meschke's and Müllenhoff's) work. The highly nationalistic, pan-German model of the interwar period, while not articulated in the same extreme manner as before, has yet to be superseded.

German-language writers made use of English and other British sword dance material in a variety of ways, mostly rather muddled. Their understanding of British society and geography tended to be very uncertain. Wolfram seems to have been relatively well informed, since he knew English well and visited England in 1935, at the time of the London international folk dance festival. Meschke was less knowledgeable though he incorporated Sharp's work in his study as examples of 'peasant (*bäuerlich*) sword dance'. Both Meschke and Wolfram seem to have had some degree of contact with Rolf Gardiner, which is not surprising since Gardiner spoke German fluently and often travelled in Germany and Austria.

Conclusions

In the English-speaking world, writers on the history and significance of sword dancing only began to move beyond the 'ancient ritual survival' thesis in the 1960s–80s. This progress was not led by academically trained scholars; rather, it was led by practical-minded teachers and enthusiasts – such as Ivor Allsop, Bill Cassie, E.C. Cawte, Roy Dommett, and Trevor Stone – who investigated actual performance practices and personal or family connections in the world of English long sword and rapper dance. Subsequently, historians and social scientists from both British and U.S. universities introduced professional and comprehensive research methodologies. The most notable examples in the larger field of the folk dance 'revival', are Georgina Boyes, Theresa Buckland, Keith Chandler, Stephen Corrsin, John Forrest, Mike Heaney, and Roy Judge. While Corrsin is the only one to produce a monograph devoted to the topic of sword dance, these writers, and others, have drawn inspiration and insight from one another's work.[26] German-language work directly on sword dance, as noted above, has hardly moved beyond Wolfram's domina-

tion. However, a great deal of exciting and innovative work
has been done in related fields, such as the great Shrovetide
celebrations which have provided the context for so much of
sword dance history on the Continent.

It is significant that scholars in the English – and German-
speaking countries alike have, from the 1960s on, convincing-
ly criticised the very bases of the collecting and interpreting
work that folklore studies developed from, and indeed have
completely recast the arguments over 'tradition' and 'folklore'. One of the most notable and often cited collections of
articles in this regard is the 1983 book edited by English historians Eric Hobsbawm and Terence Ranger, with the extraordinarily resonant title, *The Invention of Tradition*. The key
point in their argument is that we must examine the extent to
which many traditions (not just folklore, but, to take an
example from their book, traditions linked to royalty) are
recent inventions, created to meet contemporary needs.
These invented traditions 'normally attempt to establish continuity with a suitable historic past ... However ... the pecu-
liarity of 'invented' traditions is that the continuity with it
[the past] is largely factitious ... Adaptation took place for old
uses in new conditions and by using old models for new
purposes.'[27]

A topic of great importance in German-language folklore
and historical studies in general is that of continuity,
Kontinuität, in German culture, politics, and society. Because
of the terrible legacy of National Socialism, in fact, this question can turn up in practically any field. The idea of continuity has been, at certain times, enormously powerful in
German thought and writing. In brief, this is the idea that
there was profound continuity in German culture (or race, or
nationality) from antiquity – starting with Tacitus' account –
to the modern day; that the German-speaking populations
experienced little or no mixing with other peoples, neither in
cultural nor biological terms; and in general that the modern
Germans (including ethnic Germans from outside Germany
proper) were to be identified with their ancient ancestors.

In the first half of the twentieth century, when the concept
of 'Germanic continuity' reached its apogee, or perhaps its
nadir, it also proved to be an extraordinarily flexible idea.
Evidence from individual neighbouring countries was used,
in the most haphazard, erratic, and selective way, as support-

Baden-Württemberg Sword Dancers, Germany, dancing
at Whitby International Sword Dancing Festival 2000.

Photo Stephen Corrsin

ing elements for 'Germanic continuity'. This was done with
utter disregard for the unities of time, place, and actors. It is
of considerable interest that one of the most extreme scholarly spokesmen for 'Germanic continuity' in the Nazi era was
Otto Höfler, Wolfram's close friend and professional associate. Höfler proclaimed a biological function for the transmis-
sion of culture, a piece of patent nonsense which fit neatly in
National Socialism. Since the Second World War, the idea of
'Germanic continuity' from antiquity to the modern day has
been discredited by scholars.

In the field of *Volkskunde*, some particularly profound
studies have been produced by one of the outstanding
German scholars of the field, Hermann Bausinger.
Bausinger's most important monograph available in English
is *Folk Culture in a World of Technology*, the 1990 translation of
his 1961 book, *Volkskultur in der technischen Welt*. The editor,
Dan Ben-Amos, comments in the translation's foreword:

> [Bausinger] proposes a theory of expansion,
> rather than disintegration, of traditional culture
> in an age of technology ... Tradition is not passed
> on from generation to generation in language, art,
> and music as a time-honored body of knowledge
> and values. Rather, it is in a constant state of dis-
> array, about to disintegrate under the pressures of
> change; and members of the society strive to
> restore and maintain it in new rituals, displays,
> and diverse forms of entertainment – constructed
> and if necessary invented – or the revival of old
> ones. Bausinger anticipated Eric Hobsbawm and
> Terence Ranger (the editors of *The Invention of
> Tradition*) ... by considering tradition not as a cul-
> tural given but as a cultural construct ... This is
> not an entropic expansion into nothingness but a
> broadening of the communal scope of folklore
> into a diversified and complex set of relations:
> Bausinger explores them in terms of their spatial,
> temporal, and social dimensions ... Befittingly,
> one of the final reincarnations of folklore in the
> modern world is as a marketable commodity ...
> The commodification of folklore, [is] known as
> folklorism.'[28]

With these ideas – the invention of tradition, the abandon-ment of the idea of continuity, and the commodification of folklore – I conclude this essay on the historiography of sword dancing in the English- and German-speaking lands.

Notes

1. E.K. Chambers, *The Mediaeval Stage* (Mineola, N.Y.: Dover, 1996; reprint of 1903 ed.), I, p. vi.
2. *Ibid.*, I, p. 182.
3. Robert Ackerman, *The Myth and Ritual School: J. G. Frazer and the Cambridge Ritualists* (New York: Garland, 1991), pp. 199–200.
4. Cecil J. Sharp, *The Sword-Dances of Northern England: Together with the Horn Dance of Abbots Bromley* (London: English Folk Dance & Song Soc., 1985), I, pp. 10–11; originally published in three separate volumes (London: Novello, 1911–13).
5. *Ibid.*, I, 15.
6. Theresa Buckland, 'English Folk Dance Scholarship: A Review,' in Theresa Buckland, ed., *Traditional Dance: Vol. I* (Crewe: Crewe & Alsager College of Higher Education, 1982), p. 9.
7. Sharp, *Sword-Dances*, III, pp. 10, 12.
8. Chambers, *Mediaeval Stage*, I, p. 195.
9. *Ibid.*, I, p. 203. Frazer drew a great deal of material from Mannhardt and acknowledged his intellectual debt. His discussion of dances seems almost to have been paraphrased from Mannhardt. See Frazer, *The Golden Bough: A Study in Magic and Religion*, 3rd ed. (London: Macmillan, 1913), IX, pp. 238–52; and Wilhelm Mannhardt, *Der Baumkultus der Germanen und ihrer Nachbarstämme: Mythologische Untersuchungen* (Berlin: Borntraeger, 1875), pp. 540–65.
10. Chambers, *Mediaeval Stage*, I, p.183.
11. *Journal of Hellenic Studies*, 26 (1906), 191–206.
12. *Ibid.*, p.203. Dawkins' last comment refers to the widespread but unfounded assumption that cultural and ethnic 'isolation' leads to 'survivals' —more than, for instance in this case, might be found in larger towns, or ethnically Greek villages in Greece proper. There is no explanation as to why this should be so, or for that matter, why isolation should not lead to the loss of such 'survivals'.
13. *Ibid.*, p. 200.
14. Sharp, *Sword-Dances*, III, pp. 13–16.
15. *Ibid.*, III, pp. 15–16.
16. For a listing of the more important works by these (and many other) authors, see Stephen D. Corrsin, *Sword Dancing in Britain: An Annotated Bibliography*. Based on the *Holdings of the Vaughan Williams Memorial Library of EFDSS* (2nd ed., revised and expanded; London: Vaughan Williams Memorial Library, 2000.) (http://www.efdss.org/sword.htm).
17. Müllenhoff's main work on this topic is: 'Über den Schwerttanz,' *Festgaben für Gustav Homeyer zum XXVIII Juli MDCCCLXXI* (Berlin: Weidmann, 1871), pp.109–47; he published two briefer articles in 1875–76. It is of interest that Mannhardt dedicated his *Baumkultus* to Müllenhoff, his more senior professional colleague.
18. Tacitus, *Historical Works* (London: Dent, 1932), II, p. 326.
19. The literature on Tacitus' *Germania*, chiefly in German, is immense. Examples of recent essays most relevant to this study are: Manfred Fuhrmann, 'Die

Germania des Tacitus und das deutsche Nationalbewusstsein,' in Manfred
Fuhrmann, *Brechungen: Wirkungsgeschichtliche Studien zur antik-europäischen
Bildungstradition* (Stuttgart: Klett-Cotta, 1982), pp. 113–28; Volker Losemann,
'Aspekte der nationalsozialistischen Germanenideologie,' in Peter Kneissl and
Volker Losemann, ed, *Alte Geschichte und Wissenschaftsgeschichte: Festschrift für
Karl Christ zum 65. Geburtstag* (Darmstadt: Wissenschaftliche
Buchgesellschaft, 1988), pp. 256-84; and Herbert W. Benario, 'Tacitus'
Germania and Modern Germany,' *Illinois Classical Studies*, 15 (1990), 163–75.

20. See Hans Naumann, *Primitive Gemeinschaftskultur: Beiträge zur Volkskunde und
Mythologie* (Jena: Diederichs, 1921) and *Grundzüge der deutschen Volkskunde*
(Leipzig: Quelle & Meyer, 1929).

21. Paul Jacques Bloch, 'Der deutsche Volkstanz der Gegenwart,' *Hessische Blätter
für Volkskunde*, 25 (1926), 124-80 and 26 (1927), 26–80. For Wolfram's attack, see
his, 'Volkstanz, nur gesunkenes Kulturgut?' *Zeitschrift für Volkskunde*, n.F. 3
(1931), pp.26–42.

22. Kurt Meschke, *Schwerttanz and Schwerttanzspiel im germanischen Kulturkreis*
(Leipzig: Teubner, 1931.)

23. The literature on sword dancing under National Socialism in Germany and
Austria is part of the field of academic folklore (*Volkskunde*) in the same era.
Richard Wolfram has come to be seen increasingly as an important and
controversial figure in the history of German-language *Volkskunde* of the
1930s–80s, particularly in Austria. The scholarly literature referring to his
career is growing rapidly. A very important collection on the general topic is
James R. Dow and Hannjost Lixfeld, ed., *The Nazification of an Academic
Discipline: Folklore in the Third Reich* (Bloomington, Ind.: Indiana University
Press, 1994); particularly relevant are the articles by Olaf Bockhorn, Wolfgang
Emmerich, and Anka Oesterle. Wolfram's most important single work
remains, *Schwerttanz und Männerbünde* (Kassel: Barenreiter, 1936–38). Otto
Höfler's major work is *Kultische Geheimbünde der Germanen* (Frankfurt Main:
Diesterweg, 1934); only vol. 1 was ever published. Höfler's career has produced
a sizable literature in Germany. Two recent studies of his views on 'Germanic
continuity' and related specific topics are: Jan Hirschbiegel, 'Die "germanische
Kontinuitätstheorie" Otto Höflers,' *Zeitschrift der Gesellschaft für Schleswig-
Holsteinische Geschichte*, 117 (1992), 181–98; and Harm-Peer Zimmermann,
'Männerbund und Totenkult: Methodologische und ideologische Grundlinien
der Volks- und Altertumskunde Otto Höflers 1933–1945,' *Kieler Blätter für
Volkskunde*, 26 (1994), 5–27. As a topic in German historiography, 'continuity'
originally referred to the transition from the Roman Empire to the early
medieval period. Lily Weiser's main work is her *Altgermanische Junglingsweihen
und Männerbünde: Ein Beitrag zur deutschen und nordischen Altertums- und
Volkskunde* (Buhl: Konkordia, 1927). On her life and career, see Christina Niem,
'Lily Weiser-Aall (1898–1937): ein Beitrag zur Wissenschaftsgeschichte der
Volkskunde,' *Zeitschrift für Volkskunde* (1998), 25–52. A fascinating collection on
the theme of 'male bonding' is Gisela Volger and Karen von Welck, ed.,
Männerbände, Männerbünde: Zur Rolle des Mannes im Kulturvergleich (Köln:
Rautenstrauch-Joest-Museum, 1990). It should be understood that the works
cited here are only a tiny fraction of the German-language literature on
Wolfram, Höfler, Weiser, Rudolf Much, academic folklore under the Nazis,
'Germanic continuity', and 'male bonding'.

24. Wolfram, *Schwerttanz*, p.3.

25. Wolfram's articles in English are both in the *Journal of the English Folk Dance
and Song Society*: 'Sword Dances and Secret Societies,' 1 (Dec. 1932), 34–41 and

'Ritual and Dramatic Associations of Sword and Chain Dances,' 2 (1935), 35–41.
26. The works by these authors listed in my bibliography (see n.16) should be consulted, and also in Mike Heaney, *An Introductory Bibliography on Morris Dancing*, 2d ed. (London: Vaughan Williams Memorial Library, 1995).
27. Eric Hobsbawm and Terence Ranger, ed., *The Invention of Tradition* (Cambridge: Cambridge University Press, 1983), pp. 1–2, 4–5.
28. Hermann Bausinger, *Folk Culture in a World of Technology* (Bloomington, Ind.: Indiana University Press, 1990); see the 'Foreword' by Dan Ben-Amos, pp.vii–viii. For discussions of 'continuity' in Volkskunde, see Bausinger's, 'Zur Algebra der Kontinuität,' in Hermann Bausinger and Wolfgang Brückner, ed, *Kontinuität? Geschichtlichkeit und Dauer als volkskundliches Problem* (Berlin: E. Schmidt, 1969), pp.9–30; and Wolfgang Emmerich, 'The Mythos of Germanic Continuity,' in Dow and Lixfeld, ed., *Nazification*, pp.34–54.

Further reading

Corrsin, *Sword Dancing in Europe*, is a substantial historical survey of the topic. See also his, *Sword Dancing in Britain: An Annotated Bibliography*, projected as an ongoing online bibliography, regularly updated. It chiefly covers British material but includes a section on continental dancing. Ivor Allsop's collection, *Longsword Dances from Traditional and Manuscript Sources*, edited by Anthony G. Barrand (Brattleboro, VT, 1996), pulls together information and instructions on British dances, with additional material. Those interested in following new developments and information on English sword dancing should read *Rattle Up My Boys: A Quarterly Publication for Those with an Interest in Sword Dancing*, published by Trevor Stone, and *The Nut,* published by Vince Rutland. Stone maintains close contacts with continental sword dancers, and both he and Rutland have been active in organising the three biennial international sword dance festivals already held in the north-east of England in 1996–2000.

The most important German-language surveys remain Meschke's *Schwerttanz und Schwerttanzspiel*, and Wolfram's *Schwerttanz und Männerbünde*. We can only hope that some scholar in central Europe takes up the task. Dow and Lixfeld's collection, *Nazification of an Academic Discipline*, is an excellent place to start for anyone interested in the larger context of the field of German-language *Volkskunde* in the first half of the twentieth century. There appear to be no German-language periodicals in the field. An Austrian Web site on 'Schwerttanz' can be found at: http://www.fff.at/fff/dance/dances/schwert/

The linguistically adventurous should also track down a

Dutch-language periodical, published by the leading Belgian authority and the single most important figure in linking continental sword dance groups, Renaat van Craenenbroeck: *'t Zweertdanserke: het babbelblad van dansgroep Lange Wapper* (*The Little Sword Dancer: the newsletter of the Lange Wapper dance group*).

Britannia Coco-Nut Dancers in Bacup, Lancashire

Photo: Homer Sykes/Network Photographers

'In a word, we are unique': Ownership and control in an English dance custom

Theresa Buckland

When Cecil Sharp toured parts of England during the early 1900s in search of folk songs and dances, he, and others like him, viewed their mission as the restoration of a national culture to a people long alienated from their native roots. Even though these collectors were to record forms characteristic of particular regions or indeed material regarded as the personal property of certain individuals, such was their zeal to effect a nationwide revival, that questions of ownership and control of the songs and dances were rarely addressed. Indeed, ownership and control were perceived as problems for warring factions within the folk revival itself rather than as ethical concerns between the collector and his or her informant.[1]

In many cases, the singer or dancer was only too pleased to receive national recognition of the value of their songs and dances and were themselves instrumental in transmitting their knowledge for national consumption and performance. With few exceptions, this was to be the pattern of collection in the years following Sharp's death in 1924. Songs and dances regardless of where they were performed when collected were perceived by the folk revival as belonging to the nation and therefore performance rights were viewed as being held in common. The guardian of the folk revival, the English Folk Dance Society, established in 1911 by Sharp and his followers, continued to promote the practice of collected songs

and dances on a national basis through its teaching and publications, even when a particular dance or song was still current in its place of collection. This paper examines the
interaction of the Society with a particular group of dancers
who objected to this appropriation of their traditional
repertoire.

In 1929, Sharp's amanuensis, Maud Karpeles, attempted
to collect the tradition of the Britannia Coco-Nut Dancers of
Bacup, Rossendale, Lancashire. Here was an annual custom,
performed by nine men every Eastertide through the streets
of the urban and industrial Rossendale Valley. Their repertoire consisted of five dances performed with half-hoop garlands and a 'coconut dance' which could be performed either
in a linear or quadrille formation. The custom appeared to
Karpeles to be a unique phenomenon, distinguished, in dress,
by the black faces and short kilt, and, in dance form, by the
pieces of wood, known as 'coconuts' or 'nuts' which the men
tapped together as they danced. Karpeles was bemused by
this tradition but the dance's local recognition as an old custom, its special date of performance, its use of implements, its
performance by men, and its traditional route all suggested
that here was another, if highly localised, form of English ritual dance, similar to morris dancing. Already the morris
dance had been hailed by the early folk dance collectors as a
native form and thus rightfully the property of the English
nation. However, unlike most of her collecting trips,
Karpeles's attempt to record the whole repertoire seems not
to have been greeted with unqualified enthusiasm by the
dancers.

Although other coconut dance teams had existed in the
area before the First World War,[2] the Britannia Coco-Nut
Dancers (themselves a local revival of the early 1920s) were
now the only ones remaining. Perhaps with more than a hint
of business acumen, the dancers realised that in their tradition they possessed a desirable commodity which, if properly
managed, only they could supply. No doubt realising the possible increase in performance opportunities which this
national, London-based organisation, which Karpeles represented, might bring, the dancers drew up an agreement with
the English Folk Dance Society.[3]

The Britannia Coco-Nut Dancers' wariness of 'being collected' appears not to have emerged from knowledge of how

Britannia Coco-Nut Dancers at Whitby Folk Festival 1988. *Photo: Kathryn Tattersall*

the repertoire of other dance teams had been treated by the Society collectors. As far as is known, the troupe had no previous contact with morris or sword dance teams whose dances had become part of the Society's literature and teachings. Instead, the most likely explanation of the Coco-Nut Dancers' cautious behaviour can be found in the team's predominant performance venues outside their annual appearance in Rossendale at Easter. Like many ceremonial dance teams of the early twentieth century, and before, their public performances were by no means restricted to a few days in the year. The Britannia Coco-Nut Dancers regularly performed at competitions in north-west England where their unusual dance and appearance found favour in the novelty sections of competitions held at summer carnivals and fetes. Here then the maintenance of rights over their material was crucial to continued success. Furthermore, in addition to the social pleasures of belonging to a team with its weekly practices at the local working men's clubs and pubs, membership of the Coco-Nut Dancers brought opportunities for travel and the gaining of prestige when entering these competitions. Such benefits were of no little significance to men whose leisure pursuits were fairly limited in choice in the 1920s and 1930s. Although skilled workers, most of the men were employed in the local slipper works, cotton and felt factories, and coal mines. Clearly, they would be reluctant to hand over these social advantages of being a coconut dancer to a national organisation which might train imitators all over the country to usurp their privileged position. Indeed, the first point of the agreement drawn up by the dancers charges the Society not to 'learn another troupe of dancers to compete against the above mentioned troupe'.

Aware that all sorts of prestigious and financial benefits might accrue to them through the preservation of their traditions, the Britannia Coco-Nut Dancers agreed to the Society's documentation of their dances and customs in return for its support in maintaining their unique status. Perhaps surprisingly the team was quite prepared to teach part or all of its dances to the Society but only if one or more of the dancers were to be invited to London, with expenses paid, in order to ensure that 'it is done in a right and satisfactory manner'. This proposal seems not to have been taken up. It is difficult, of course, to know what framework for negotiation was imposed in the unrecorded verbal exchanges which first took place between the Society's local representative and the team. The dancers' undertaking to 'maintain the Tradition at its best' and to 'make no alteration without first consulting and discussing same with the Society' sounds suspiciously like the Society's understanding of change as a degenerative feature in the operation of a tradition.

The Society was given leave by the dancers to use the record of the Britannia team in the best interests of both. Finally, and most importantly, the Society was cast in the role of patron by being required to give to the dancers 'every possible publicity and assistance'. For its part, the Society charged the team to the best of its ability to guard against anyone copying the tradition.

So in May 1929, Karpeles collected from one dancer all five garland dances and tunes together with brief historical details.[4] However, the unique coconut dance appears nowhere in her notes. Nor indeed, is there any later written record of the coconut dance in the Society's library. It would appear that the draft agreement was not fully implemented.

It is surprising then given this background to discover a press report in the *Bacup Times* of 1938 that a sound film was to be made by the Society of the team's dances 'so that they may be taught to other teams'. Was the Britannia team becoming less concerned about maintaining its monopoly? The report in the following week's press, however, after the film of the coconut dance had been shot states the purpose of the filming to be 'in order that it shall never be in danger of dying out'. Evidently though the production of the film caused some anxiety to the dancers for their leader, Arthur Bracewell, wrote to Douglas Kennedy, then director of the Society, seeking reassurance. Kennedy in his reply mentioned a previous letter (which has not survived) in which he:

> assured you that the film ... will be used for scientific purposes only and will not be subject to any form of commercial exploitation.

Here then was the agreement in operation, with the Coco-Nut Dancers decidedly nervous about the Society's intentions and apprehensive about profits disappearing into their patron's pockets.

Yet during the 1930s, the team was able to call upon the

Society to give the promised 'assistance' when questions on the competition circuit were raised as to whether the coconut dance was a genuine Morris dance. Kennedy duly furnished a letter in support, authenticating the dance as a true Morris Coconut Dance.[5] But the prime support of the Society resulted from the increase in more prestigious engagements for the team. Top of the list were performances at the Royal Albert Hall in London at which they first appeared in 1931. This practice continued on a fairly regular basis of every three to five years until the Society's cessation of these concerts in 1984. In addition to this, other Society events also included district gatherings and concerts, followed by festivals from the 1950s onwards. The growing fame of the dancers then led to radio and TV appearances.

Reluctance to place the whole repertoire on visual record continued after the Second World War. One dancer of the 1950s recalled the team's deliberate performance of only parts of the dance so that it could not be copied. Local pride and the desire to maintain control are revealed in his statement that:

> it's a traditional Lancashire dance and we want to keep it, we don't want it taking elsewhere. I mean if they get a set of dances they'll get more engagements than we will.[6]

'They' in this quotation refers to the Society, which appeared to threaten the team's unique position by filming their dances in order to copy them. In 1981 Douglas Kennedy recalled that when a Society film of the team was made in 1951 he was asked by the dancers to destroy his notes on the tradition, a request which he honoured.[7] The colour film interestingly enough does not present the two formations of the Coco-Nut Dance in their entirety but instead merges the quadrille formation into the linear form of the dance with no warning. Editing questions may indeed have taken precedence here but any question of the ownership of the coconut dance is firmly settled by the film credits which state that copyright is held by the team.

Fear that the Society would assert control over the dance if the Britannia team failed to maintain the tradition was voiced in 1954 on the retirement of long-serving dancers, Arthur Bracewell and Mark Pilling. The latter urged young members 'to carry on and keep the dance going. If you do not, the people in the South will take hold of it.'[8] This exhortation was felt necessary even though the Society's local representative had told the gathering that:

> [The] Nutters have something which is so special that none of us in the Society have ever dared to imitate or copy it.[9]

Certainly, the Society has never included the team's choreographic and musical repertoire within their teaching courses and publications.

The 1929 agreement binds the Coco-Nut Dancers themselves to take all reasonable precautions against imitation. During one performance prior to the mid 1950s, the concertina player reputedly thwarted an audience member's attempt to notate the tune of the Nut Dance, known officially as the 'Tip Toe Polka' (or more familiarly as 'Clough Bang') by switching to the alternative melody of 'Shooting Star'.[10] Another concertina player's daughter recalled the restrictions placed on herself by her father. When she hummed the infectious 'Tip Toe Polka' in the house, her father would say: 'ah, you can hum that in here, but you just forget it when you go out'.[11] The dancers insist that the music is copyright, great trust being placed in the 1929 agreement by the older members of the team.

Yet with a growing number of visitors to their traditional performances on Easter Saturday, composed mainly of enthusiasts for English traditional dance and music, measures to hinder any attempt to note the repertoire have obviously been more difficult to initiate and sustain. In any case, by the 1970s the dancers' increased media exposure in the national press, in popular books on traditional customs of England, in features on radio and on TV had firmly established the Britannia Coco-Nut Dancers as a unique phenomenon. If anything, the number of film and video cameras apparent at Easter during the 1980s was perhaps viewed more as a compliment than as a menace to their position. Thus the threat of imitators has lessened as time has gone by but still the dancers can be alert to maintaining the agreement between themselves and the Society. When the 'Tip Toe Polka' was used by an outsider to accompany a song about the team in 1976, the dancers wrote to the Society to disassociate themselves from it.[12] Yet imitation of the tune can occasionally be heard in the pubs where the dancers perform on Easter Saturday, as members of the folk revival scene assemble to play and sing. Indeed, the tune, simple and catchy, has often been included in the repertoire of various folk revival musicians. Its appearance in print, when it comes to the Coco-Nut Dancers' notice, however, seems to prompt a different response, particularly when their name is directly associated with the copy.

Duplication of the tradition may not always be a danger from outside of course. In order to prevent other teams being spawned from the parent body, each new dancer must sign a small typed piece of paper which binds him to the Society agreement. It is signed when the others judge it likely that the novice will graduate into the team. The Nut Dance is certainly distinctive and more difficult to learn than most other English ceremonial dances, which leads older dancers, in particular, to believe that even with a visual record, it is impossible for anyone to imitate the dance from film. Only through participant knowledge does the real threat of duplication appear to exist. At an informal level, further control is maintained through the dancers' recruitment policy. Although entry requirements to the team are never overtly stated, it is clear on examining the team's composition over the years, that certain factors are common. All (apart from a recent exception) have been born and bred in the Rossendale Valley, have worked relatively locally since leaving school, are married and mostly over thirty years old. It is particularly apparent at practice nights that the men share a common local cultural experience when their conversation tends to centre on events in the valley. Into this ostensibly loose but actually tightly defined social group, any aspiring dancer has to demonstrate his right to belong. In a subtle manner, the Coco-Nut Dancers ensure that control lays exclusively with the existing team, particularly with its older members. The team remains suspicious of any outside interest which threatens to undermine its independent control.

> That's the reason why I think the Nutters have gone on so long. We've never let outsiders take us over and what we've done has always been by general agreement. Never let outsiders interfere![13]

Attempts to capitalise on the team's unique appeal have always been viewed with suspicion. One commercial firm wished to recruit the dancers into their advertising campaign for a brand of crisps; this would have necessitated changes to the costume. Despite the attractive financial offers made, the dancers were not at all willing to sacrifice their identity. Earlier in the team's history, the idea of becoming a professional troupe was mooted but rejected on the grounds that it would involve loss of independence since a manager would need to be appointed. Although the team has a leader, a secretary, and a treasurer, the manner of debate on practice nights with regard to future bookings is not at all formally structured. Yet, during the period of fieldwork, it was clear that there was a quiet respect for the older members of the team who held these posts. As a concertina player observed:

> I think there's quite a conscious effort not to change the existing very loose set-up, but in other ways very rigid way of discussing proposals or what events they should dance at. It's very much a democratic way of going about it.[14]

The dancers know that much of their prestige lies in their respect for tradition. Radical departures from convention will not work to the team's advantage, although by no means is the attitude so self-conscious that it promotes a fascination with uncovering 'Ur'-forms of behaviour and dress. It is the interpersonal and local contact which is valued rather than the written historical record.

For the most part, the English Folk Dance and Song Society's interaction with the Britannia Coco-Nut Dancers has not been of a dictatorial nature. Although Douglas Kennedy provided an origin legend which the team has seen fit to repeat when an explanation of their activity is needed, the Society has acted primarily as a promotional agent. An exception however has been the Society's attitude towards one particular dance in the repertoire. During the late 1970s and early 1980s, Garland Dance Number Four was rarely performed in public. Reasons cited by the dancers were the number of turns in the dance, the relationship of the music to the dance and the solo part which they felt uneasy performing in a repertoire which otherwise places so much emphasis on group movement. The over-riding concern, however, was 'they say it's modern'. 'They', so often used to mean outsiders to the tradition here seemed to mean former dancers. Yet it appears from oral evidence that a dance known as Garland Dance Number Four was performed by the Britannia team's predecessors, who transmitted the whole of their repertoire after the First World War. Further light was thrown on the view of the dance's modernity in the manuscripts of Frederick Hamer, a Morris dancer and collector of traditional practices.[15] In 1950, Hamer visited the Britannia Coco-Nut Dancers' practice and noted:

> the 4th, it was explained to me, was never done on E.F.D.S. occasions since Douglas (Kennedy) has requested them to leave it out. He says 'it's too modern' according to Norman W. (dancer since the 1920s). Perhaps that is because they use a waltz step for it.

Whether or not the dancers of the 1950s disliked the dance on aesthetic grounds is impossible to determine but the influence of Kennedy on the team's selection of dances for performance is noteworthy. Modernity clearly did not square with the Society's view of ancient English tradition. Control here was being exercised by the Society and yet Garland Dance Number Four remains in the team's repertoire today.

What emerges clearly from the study of the 1929 agreement and its impact is the mutually beneficial effect for the Britannia Coco-Nut Dancers and the English Folk Dance Society. The Society could point to a unique ancient tradition, virtually without parallel which could be displayed at its celebrations of regional and national folk culture. The gains for the Britannia team were perhaps more impressive. Indeed, it could be argued that the patronage of the Society guaranteed the continuity of the tradition. Through its provision of performance venues on a countrywide network and granting of academic credence to the custom as a genuine relic of national significance, the Society boosted the dancers' importance within their own community and pushed them into the national limelight.

This was achieved despite or perhaps because of a number of potential tensions within the interaction. On the one hand, the Society represented a culture which was national in its focus, middle-class, southern, intellectual and elitist. On the other hand, the Coco-Nut Dancers emerged from a local, working-class, northern, non-intellectual and popular culture. In the meeting of these two worlds, the dancers, seemingly disadvantaged in terms of power relations, asserted their customary rights to ownership and control of their performance and, in retaining independence, gained a kudos, which would grow with time, as the only surviving examples of their type. 'In a Word We Are Unique' concludes the Britannia Coco-Nut Dancers' recent publicity hand-out; but it is a uniqueness achieved through a timely and astute response to the folk paradigm of the early twentieth century.

Notes

This paper was originally presented at the Second British-Swedish Conference on Musicology: Ethnomusicology, Cambridge, 5–10 August 1989.
I wish to thank the Britannia Coco-Nut Dancers without whose patience and generous help this paper would not have been possible; also grateful thanks to A E Green, formerly of the Institute of Dialect and Folk Life Studies, University of Leeds.

1. For aspects of the debate see Roy Judge, 'Mary Neal and the Esperance Morris,' *Folk Music Journal* 5:5 (1989), 545–91.
2. Theresa Buckland, 'The Tunstead Mill Nutters of Rossendale, Lancashire,' *Folk Music Journal*, 5:2 (1986), 132–49.
3. The drafts of this agreement are housed in the Vaughan Williams Memorial Library, Cecil Sharp House, 2 Regent's Park Road, London.
4. Deposited in the Vaughan Williams Memorial Library, London.
5. Copy in the possession of the Britannia Coco-Nut Dancers.
6. Interview with Mr H Woodrup, Stacksteads, Bacup, 25 April 1979.
7. Douglas Kennedy, personal correspondence with author, 8 June 1981.
8. *Bacup Times*, 8 May 1954, p.8.
9. *Ibid.*
10. Interview with Mr L. Pilling, Nantwich, Cheshire, 15 April 1978.
11. Interview with Mrs E. Caygill, Bacup, 22 August 1978.
12. Interview with Mr B. Daley, Britannia, Bacup, 11 July 1978.
13. *Ibid.*
14. Interview with Mr I. O'Brien, Tyldesley, Manchester, 28 April 1982.
15. Housed in the Vaughan Williams Memorial Library, London.

Little Downham (Cambridgeshire) Molly dancers,
Plough Monday, 1932. George Prigg (cadger), George
Green (button accordion). *Credit: William Palmer.*

Molly dancing: A study of discontinuity and change

Elaine Bradtke

In eighteenth century England, agricultural workers in East Anglia often engaged in winter time street performances that became known as Molly dancing. These dancers disguised themselves and went around their home region, performing versions of local social dances in exchange for largesse. They were often destructive, drunk and disreputable in appearance. The Molly dancers were more feared than respected and their dances were viewed as degenerate by early twentieth century collectors. Due to changes in rural life, social reforms, and wartime fatalities, Molly dancing died out in the 1930s.

During the 1970s, the English Folk Revival experienced a dramatic expansion. The newcomers that swelled the ranks were often interested in little-known genres previously ignored. As part of this fascination with the obscure, the Molly genre became a candidate for revival. The first performances of the revived dances took place in the late 1970s. In the decades that followed, many have learned the small number of collected dances, or developed their own repertoire loosely based on the older genre. The number of Molly dancers seems to be steadily rising, and with this growth in numbers, the diversity of performance style and the repertoire of dances has also increased. One wonders if a nineteenth century Molly dancer, presented with the spectacles of today would recognise them as being the same form. With such a wide range of expression, audiences and dancers alike find it increasingly difficult to answer the question 'what is Molly dancing?' It is the intent of this article to help clear up some of this confusion.

This study is based on archival and field research conducted both in England and the United States, including, interviews, direct observation, participation, questionnaires, video and audio taped performances, photographs, and dance and musical analysis. Historical accounts of pre-revival dancers, and the results of a survey of contemporary Molly dancers were used as a basis for comparison. This brought to light not only the variations in contemporary practices which range from traditionalist to innovative, but how they in turn differ from their late nineteenth and early twentieth century predecessors.

Molly dancing as it was

The history of Molly dancing is not well documented. Very little is known about its origins, though the performances were in many ways similar to peasant riots and rough music. Molly dancing was one of the many forms of house-to-house visitation in the expectation of largesse that were once common in England. Much of what is known about the performance of Molly dancing in the late nineteenth and early twentieth century was gathered by the dancer/collectors Russell Wortley, Cyril Papworth, William Palmer, Joseph Needham and Arthur Peck. Additional information has been extracted from newspaper archives by George Frampton.

The area that includes the counties of Norfolk, Suffolk, Cambridgeshire, together with parts of Hertfordshire, Bedfordshire, Lincolnshire and Essex, is commonly known as East Anglia and the Fens. Historical references to Molly dancing are concentrated in this agricultural region. Here too over the centuries, the celebration of Plough Monday (the first Monday after Twelfth Night – 6 January) was a common occurrence. Molly dancers were usually agricultural workers who existed on the edge of starvation. Any misfortune, ill health or bad weather that prevented them from going out to work made life all the more miserable for them and their families. The performances of the Molly dances dances occurred during the Christmas season, on Boxing Day or Plough Monday. The period between Christmas and Plough Monday was an unpaid holiday for agricultural labourers, who used

these outings as a way to earn some money, as well as a diver-
sion from their hardships. Sometimes, if the winter was particularly bad, they would dance out on more than one day
during the season. They usually spent the day touring around
their own and neighbouring villages. On Plough Monday,
many Molly dancers would make their way to Cambridge
itself to dance and collect money. In the evening, they
returned to their home village for a meal, and sometimes a little impromptu social dancing in the pub.

The dancers disguised themselves with black face and
women's clothing. Molly dancing was closely related to other
Plough Monday and mid-winter festivities where misrule
often reigned, and these disguises offered them some small
protection from recognition. Not only were they known to be
rowdy and destructive on their own, Molly dancers often
associated with plough gangs. These were groups of young
men who went round the village with a plough, stopping at a
house or business to ask for money, and threatening to dam-
age the property if none was forthcoming. This practice
derives from a pre-Reformation custom, in which the plough
gangs would raise money for the church. After the
Reformation (during which such frivolous activities were
banned), Plough Monday faded from the church calendar.
But customs die hard, and Plough Monday continued to be
celebrated outside of the church. By the nineteenth century,
plough gangs and Molly dancers divided their take among
themselves, or gave to local charities, poor widows and other
needy neighbours, instead of making religious offerings.

The Molly dancers not only set out to collect money during the Christmas season (though this was an important
aspect). Their seasonal appearances had an implied message,
a reminder that as low as they were in the social hierarchy, the
local economy depended on their work. That the actions of
Molly dancers and plough gangs were tolerated is part of the
legacy of the relationship between the labourers and land
owners. As Stephen Nissenbaum writes:

> Much of the seasonal excess that took place at
> Christmas was not merely chaotic 'disorder' but
> behavior that took a profoundly ritualized form.
> Most fundamentally, Christmas was an occasion
> when the social hierarchy itself was symbolically
> turned upside down, in a gesture that inverted

designated roles of gender, age, and class.[1]

Plough Monday became a time for the ploughboys to vent their frustration, get even with wrongdoers and have a little spree while the authorities looked the other way. It was part of the accepted celebratory excess found during the Christmas season in early modern England.

From time to time the confused notion circulates that Molly dancing is really a degraded form of Cotswold, or south Midland morris.[2] In fact, the Molly dances were parodies of ordinary social dances, performed to well-known tunes. When the cultural context, choreography and musical accompaniment of the Molly dances is looked at with a critical eye, it soon becomes clear that the Molly dances were distinct in appearance, repertoire, and season of performance.

In almost every description of Molly dancers, at least some of the dancers were said to be wearing women's clothing. Depending on the group, one man might be elaborately costumed as the 'lady' with a veil, gown, bonnet, and petticoats. In other groups several men would wear borrowed skirts with perhaps a bonnet or shawl. It is this habit of wearing feminine clothing that resulted in the Cambridgeshire press applying the term 'Molly' to these dancers in the mid-1860s. Molly was a derogative term used to describe a male with feminine attributes, and sometimes included homosexuals.

The other dancers wore everyday clothes with ribbons and rosettes attached to their shirts, sashes, and festive (often top) hats. A few groups were recorded as taking special care with their appearance, wearing sashes or baldrics in specific colours to indicate their particular village. Other groups wore a motley assortment of clothing, with strips of ribbons or fabric attached to their sleeves and sometimes their trousers.

The Molly dancers often blackened their faces, ranging from smudges to full coverage. Their make-up consisted of burnt cork, soot, or a combination of soot and grease, items easily available in even the humblest of homes. In keeping with the behavioural standards of the nineteenth century, only men were Molly dancers. There are several recorded instances of women joining in for an occasional dance as they made their rounds, but they were not regular members of the group.

There was often one character (who accompanied the 'Lady' or Molly) known as the 'Lord'. He wore distinctive

Little Downham (Cambridgeshire) Molly dancers, Plough Monday, 1932.

Credit: Willam Palmer

clothing, often with extra sashes, or rosettes, and a different hat from the other dancers. If both a Lord and Lady were present, they would dance as the top couple in the set, leading the dance. The dancers were accompanied by non-dancing men who had specific functions. There may have been an umbrella man, who had the important task of protecting the musician from rain and snow. The musician himself was usually not one of the farm labourers, but an outsider, hired for the day. Another man would look after the dancers' coats and belongings, while they were dancing. Perhaps most important was the 'cadger', who was trusted with the money box. He often wore a distinct costume from the others. The 'sweeper' or 'whiffler' carried a broom or other implement and cleared a space in the crowd for the dancers, or swept away the snow.

The earliest detailed accounts of Molly dancers are found in nineteenth century newspapers. In the Cambridge papers, there are references to Molly dancers from about 1826 to the turn of the century. The contemporary articles were full of derision. Some examples given by Frampton described them as 'Bedizened in faded finery and dancing to anything but sweet music'[3] or, 'truculent rustics dressed in an outlandish and savage guise, who paraded in companies of six or eight and after executing a wild and somewhat terrific kind of dance, surrounded passengers and made violent incursions into shops demanding money.'[4]

As colourful as these descriptions are, they do not tell us much about the dances, but rather focus on the antics of the dancers. Many accounts dwelled on the court cases which resulted from brawls among the participants. Around Cambridge, the celebration of Plough Monday in the 1870s was fraught with violence and unruly behaviour. Molly dancers from villages surrounding Cambridge converged on the market place for some impromptu competitive dancing. Cambridge was a relatively lucrative place for them to perform, compared to their home villages. Each team would stake out a territory in the town to dance and collect money. Fights would break out between rival groups claiming the same area. Within their own villages, Molly dancers were blamed for the destruction of property, such as broken windows and damaged fences.

However, not all Plough Monday events were riotous. In some villages, from about 1863 to World War I, groups of chil-

dren went from house to house in a form of Molly dancing
while the menfolk were at work. When the weather was unfit
for ploughing, or times were hard, the men would come out
instead of the children.[5]

The dances and music

The Molly dances were ignored by Cecil Sharp and his contemporaries because they obviously derived from the social
dances, many of which had already been collected. In this
regard, the Molly dances differ from the other English display dances,[6] all of which developed repertoires independent
of the social dances. The disorderly reputation of the dancers
themselves did little to entice the collectors. There was no
real interest in collecting the Molly dances, until the 1930s.
By this time, there had been no dancing for decades in most
of the East Anglian villages and the collectors had to rely on
the few surviving dancers and the memories of elderly people.

One example of this is Cyril Papworth's collection of
feast dances obtained from some of his older relatives who
lived in Comberton. These were social dances popular in
rural districts and were often called 'country dances' by the
urban-based collectors. What Papworth collected as feast
dances formed the basis for the repertoire of the Comberton
Molly dancers. Similar local dances would have been used by
Molly dancers from other villages. In addition, the
Comberton Molly dancers had a dance of their own which
they called the 'Special Molly'. This was related in style to the
feast dances, but only the Molly dancers performed it. In
describing this type of dance, Cecil Sharp writes that they are
'the ordinary, everyday dance of the country-folk, performed
not merely on festal days, but whenever opportunity offered
and the spirit of merrymaking was abroad'.[7] According to
Sharp 'The steps and figures are simple and easily learned, so
that anyone of ordinary intelligence and of average physique
can without difficulty qualify as a competent performer.'[8] The
repertoire was limited and familiar and the footwork was simple and natural.

The dances themselves consisted of unsophisticated, easily learned and remembered choreography. They were usually
danced in longways sets (two parallel lines of dancers,
arranged with partners facing each other). The top couple led
the dance, interacting with the other couples as they worked

their way down the set, gradually bringing everyone into the dance. The figures of the dance would be repeated until the top couple reached the bottom of the set and then made their way back up to the top. A stylistic distinction between the Molly dances and the social dances was the use of an upper-arm hold by the Molly dancers. This was instead of grasping hands or holding one's partner in ballroom position during swings. This simple expedient eliminated any potential confusion resulting from men dancing the 'lady's' part. The names of the dances often described a feature of their choreography, for example, 'Up the Middle and Down the Sides', or 'Four Hand Reel'.[9] Other names, such as 'Flowers of Edinburgh' referred to the tune commonly associated with the dance.

The music consisted of popular tunes such as 'Keel Row', 'Flowers of Edinburgh', 'Smash the Window', 'Soldier's Joy', 'Cock of the North', 'Pop Goes the Weasel' and 'The Girl I Left Behind Me'. In addition there were hornpipes, reels, jigs, and even waltzes. The musician was often a Gypsy fiddler, hired to play for the dancers (often the same person who played for the local social dances). Sometimes there would be an extra musician playing percussive instruments such as metal pots or basins, or a drum, triangle, or tambourine. During the second half of the nineteenth century, the concertina and later the accordion began to supplant the fiddle. One reason for this change was the ability of the free reed instruments to better withstand the cold and damp weather of the English midwinter.

Some aspects of nineteenth century Molly dancing were reminders of a time when peasant uprisings were a common way to gain concessions from those in power. The dance and music were secondary to the misrule and the threat of destructive behaviour. Their use of familiar tunes and local country dances, or spontaneous 'jigging about' were not signs of a degenerate tradition, but instead indicate an underlying function. These popular tunes and dances allowed them to be spontaneous, appearing with very little advance preparation. If the Molly dancers' primary impetus was to put on a good show, they would have developed specialised choreography as the other display dancers had. Instead of pretty dances, they relied on their rough appearance, unruly actions, and thinly veiled threats of violence or work stoppage to inspire generosity. In some instances, they used their licence for misrule to settle old grudges. Their disorderly behaviour was amplified by their association with plough gangs.

As the balance of power in rural areas became formalised and more people gained the right to vote, and as the welfare state arose and negated the need for communal contributions to the support of the poor, Molly dancing began to lose its meaning. Molly dancing faded out in the early part of the twentieth century, along with the other Plough Monday celebrations, having been repeatedly denigrated in the press for the drunken, violent behaviour of the participants. Change in agricultural practices, the advent of social welfare, and compulsory education all contributed to this decline. The devastation of the male population in two world wars put a final end to Molly dancing in the few villages that still kept up the tradition. By the time anyone thought to collect the dances, there was very little source material left. The result is a rather sparse repertoire preserved for future generations, at first glance not much of a foundation on which to build a revival.

What is Molly dancing now?
The revival of the Molly dances occurred almost as an afterthought. That there was little interest in these dances until the 1930s was indicative of their lack of status in the revival. Derivative of simple social dances, they were less attractive to collectors and potential performers than the more graceful Cotswold style or the intricate sword dances. The association of Molly dances with disreputable behaviour only added to their aura of degeneracy. It was only when the Molly dances had disappeared from active performance and nearly faded from memory that Joseph Needham, Arthur Peck, William Palmer, and later, Russell Wortley, and Cyril Papworth tried to salvage what could be found. Even so, there was quite a gap between the first interest in the dances and any attempt to revive them.

The first widespread interest began following a workshop given by Russell Wortley in the winter of 1977. His presentation was based on the results of his research into the Molly dances of Cambridgeshire, and the Cambridge Morris Men's early attempts at reviving the form. From there the seed was planted, though it took a while to bear any fruit. The time was ripe for something different, and it appears Molly dancing was it.

George Frampton cites the 1976 release by Ashley Hutchings and the Albion Band of Rattlebone and Ploughjack[10] as an influence on the growth of interest in the revival of both Molly and Welsh Border dances.[11] During this time, there was an underground current of disatsifaction with the state of the predominant display dance form, Cotswold morris and its 'namby-pamby hanky waving and jingling bells and flowers round your hat, etc. etc. All that jigging about like demented rabbits, leaving yourself open to ridicule and public scorn.'[12]

This sentiment fuelled an interest in some of the more obscure traditional dance forms. These genres, such as border morris (from the Welsh/English border regions) and Molly dancing (from Cambridge and surrounding East Anglia), represented a rowdier, less refined aesthetic.

A pioneering group to emerge in the nineteen-seventies was the Shropshire Bedlams, a Welsh border morris team.[13] They were brazen, creative and broke many of the unwritten rules of the earlier folk dance revival. Led by their founder, the musician John Kirkpatrick, they whooped and hollered, flailed about with sticks and created quite a stir among their fellow dancers. Inspired by the daring and flair of the Bedlams' performances and their rejection of convention, a group of former Headcorn Morris Men (who had attended the Wortley workshop) decided to form the Seven Champions Molly Dancers. Their intent was to imitate the spirit, though not the dances, of the Shropshire Bedlams.[14] In essence, the Seven Champions took the core of pre-revival Molly dances and moulded them into something radically different from the current Cotswold performance style and repertoire.

While probably the best known and most influential of the late twentieth century Molly dancers, the Seven Champions were not the first of the new wave. In fact, the Cambridge Morris Men, with the help of members Russell Wortley and Cyril Papworth, and Mepal Molly, led by Brian Cookman, were the first groups to revive Molly dancing. Both groups made their first public appearances in the winter of 1977, and they are both still active performers of Molly dances in a very traditionalist style.

The Molly dance as defined by the current dancers

In the pre-revival era, there were certain common elements between Molly and other forms of display dances, such as the occasional use of bells and handkerchiefs by the Molly dancers. During the twentieth century, the dance forms have become more segregated. Molly dancing is now consciously quite different from the Cotswold style. There is, of course, a great variety in the performance of Cotswold dances, but there are a few generalisations that may be safely made. In appearance, they tend towards white and bright coloured clothing, uniform within the group to some extent. They may wear waistcoats or baldrics, knee britches or long trousers, lightweight footwear and sometimes hats decorated with ribbons, feathers, flowers and assorted pins and badges. The choreography of the dances is complex and varied. The emphasis in their movements is upwards, realised through arm movements, leaping, and stepping lightly. Their steps are accompanied by jingle bells attached either to pads tied below the knee, or (often on women's teams) bands tied at the ankles. The hand movements are emphasised by the use of handkerchiefs that are waved in carefully co-ordinated patterns. Some dances are performed with sticks that are clashed in specific rhythmic patterns, instead of handkerchiefs.

Although the Molly dancers' costumes vary widely, there is an effort to make their appearance distinct from the Cotswold style costume, especially if they perform both types of dance. Among Molly dancers, black face, face paint or masks seem to be nearly universal. Frequently there is a man/woman or some sort of cross-dressing, though this not considered essential by all groups. If there is a man/woman, s/he is often accompanied by a 'lord' dressed in bits and pieces of formal wear. The Molly dancers avoid the white clothes, flowered hats, bells, sticks, handkerchiefs,[15] leaps and lightness associated with the Cotswold style. They generally employ simpler choreography, heavy shoes, boots or even clogs, and often carry nothing in their hands. Molly dancers favour either an English social dance style of stepping or heavier, emphatic stepping. They keep the body low to the ground, and put weight on the full foot. The attitude the Molly dancers project is more rough and wild rather than graceful. Because of the face painting, cross dressing and outlandish, mismatched clothing worn by some groups, they give an impression of being slightly deranged, and unpredictable.

In addition, most Molly groups acknowledge the roots of their dance by restricting the performance of Molly dances to the winter season, or making a point of celebrating Plough Monday or Boxing Day. Pre-Christmas shopping days and early January weekends (including the Straw Bear festival) are also popular performance dates for Molly dancers. The Cotswold morris is primarily a spring and summer dance, though there are always exceptions.

It is interesting to note that in a dance form where cross-dressing is wide-spread, we find a larger percentage of mixed gender groups compared to the rest of the English display dance scene. The Molly dances were revived at a late date in the folk dance revival, a period when women were again becoming active in the performance of display dances. Many of the people who took up Molly dancing were not sympathetic to the Morris Ring's men only rule. In addition, many mixed Molly groups evolved out of mixed gender groups who perform other display dances (and who were already considered outcasts by some). A mixed gender group that performs an allegedly debased dance form is perhaps doubly unconcerned with the status quo of the display dance revival.

Revival Molly dancing has evolved to encompass a wide range of styles. For every generalisation there is at least one exception. The choreography is usually for even numbers of dancers ranging from four to ten. Contemporary groups consist of men, women, or a mixture of both. There are also a few children's groups. The dancers' genders have little relation to their role in the dance. The new repertoire is often less closely related to social dances than the old repertoire. Now, special dances are composed with complex figures, elaborated with exaggerated arm and leg motions. There is a great deal of variation in appearance; but some cross dressing, face painting and the use of heavy footwear (often work boots) is generally present. Costumes may be quite individual or uniform depending on the group. At the end of the twentieth century, Molly dancers included university students, computer programmers, teachers, farm managers, and were drawn from the middle class. Rarely do all the members of a group live in the same village, nor are their performances always restricted to their home region.

The high point of the revival Molly season is the Straw

Bear festival (itself a revival) on the Saturday preceding Plough Monday in Whittlesey, Cambridgeshire. Some revival groups only dance during the winter, others, such as the Seven Champions, dance year round. Many groups also perform other types of English display dances during the other seasons.

Three subgroups of Molly dance

Once the Molly dance revival began in earnest, it quickly diverged into three sub-groups that span a wide range between traditionalist and innovative interpretations. Because of the different approaches, what has evolved is not a narrowly defined form. There is a great deal of diversity in costume, repertoire, performance season, choreography, music, and extra characters. Yet these groups are united in their interest in performing something different from the Cotswold style dances. At the traditionalist end are those who try to keep Molly dancing as close as possible to the original as they understand it. Emphasis is placed on re-creating the pre-revival form. Their performances are more akin to historical re-enactments rather than a living tradition. The early revival of the Molly dances was prompted by the interest in East Anglian traditions. Faced with skeletal descriptions and few collected dances, the traditionalist revivalists chose to limit their performance of this genre to specific days or seasons and a few dances rather than expand upon the repertoire. Because of the choreography's lack of complexity, many seasonal groups provide limited instruction or none at all in the performances of these dances.

An example of a traditionalist group is the Cambridge Morris Men, who only perform their Molly in the winter season and dance Cotswold-style Morris for the remainder of the year. They consider the Molly dances to be part of their repertoire of English display dances, rather than their sole reason for being. They learned the dances from a combination of archival references, articles (Needham and Peck), and other dancers via Cyril Papworth. The Cambridge Morris Men were interested in the revival of the East Anglian customs related to Plough Monday because of their geographic location. Their revival of the Molly dances was also partly sparked by the revival of the Balsham plough gang. The Cambridge Morris Men performed Molly dances in Balsham

on at least one occasion, but the villagers voiced a strong pref-
erence for the Cotswold dances. Now they tour around East
Anglian villages with their Molly dances and end the evening
in Balsham with a performance of Cotswold dances. As with
any other part of their repertoire, the Cambridge men
rehearse the Molly dances before taking them out. They perform them in a traditional manner, though they admit their
tempo might be a bit faster. The Cambridge Morris Men wear
a special costume for their Molly dancing which differs from
their regular performance garb. They do not wear black face
and they do aim for a uniform appearance. They have a
man/woman whose costume varies depending on who is
dancing the part.

Those who perform the pre-revival dances but have added
and adapted other dances in order to broaden the repertoire,
represent something of a middle ground in the revival. Their
work is based on the premise that a great deal of original
material was lost as the form died out. They attempt to recre-
ate Molly dancing in the spirit of the pre-revival form, while
allowing themselves some room for growth and development.

A team which represents this middle ground is Pig's Dyke
Molly. They started when a group of members of Yaxley
Morris (based in Peterborough area) who took up Molly dancing in 1988 because of its local connections. They learned
their first dances from members of Old Hunts Molly who
were in turn trained by Cyril Papworth in the pre-revival
repertoire. They have since added a few dances of their own.
They have minimal formal instruction in the dances before
they begin their public appearance. They perform Molly
dancing in the winter season, primarily at the Straw Bear festival and on Plough Monday. Pig's Dyke is known for individ-
ualised costumes in a black and white colour scheme. Many
of the outfits consist of eccentric pieces of unrelated clothing
(a feather boa, a sombrero, a cape, etc). There is a great deal of
cross-dressing by both sexes. Dancers of either gender wear
skirts or dresses, others leggings or trousers. They paint their
faces with white make-up, adding black designs in some
cases. Their lack of uniform appearance and minimal
rehearsal gives them a spontaneous and whimsical air.

The dancers at the innovative end of the continuum see
the Molly dance material as a basis on which to build an alternative dance form, related to, yet separate from the other

types of English display dances. This style is sometimes
known as Festival Molly, since it's proponents often develop
their performances to appeal to festival audiences. For these
groups, the creation of new dances and a recognisable team
style are vital to the process of exploration and expansion of
the Molly repertoire, for maintaining interest during year
round performances and rehearsals and for obtaining festival
bookings. The innovative groups see Molly dancing as an
opportunity to construct a genre of their own within the field
of English display dances.

The Seven Champions, fall squarely into this class. As
founding member Dave Dye said in an interview, 'We went to
a Russell Wortley workshop on Molly, which we decided was,
as it stood, extremely uninteresting stuff, and not worth the
bother of doing. But it could develop into something that was
interesting and worth doing.'[16] They did not entirely abandon
the legacy of the earlier Molly dancers. Their costume is
loosely based on the descriptions of Molly dancers from
south-west Cambridgeshire by Wortley and Papworth.[17] The
top hats with green yellow and maroon ribbons, single
maroon baldric with rosettes, white collarless shirts with the
sleeves rolled up and the dark brown corduroy trousers mark
them as the Seven Champions. Their use of lollygags (twine
tied below the knees, used by farm labourers to keep rodents
from running up the inside of their trousers), black-face and
their lack of bells and handkerchiefs distinguishes them as
Molly dancers. In addition, they had hobnails attached to
their boots, so that their footwear provides a tangible link to
the rural labourers of an earlier time. Aware of their roles as
performers they pay special attention to details from the
design of the outfits to the way they begin and end their
performances.

As pioneers, they built their initial repertoire upon the few
collected dances they were able to find in archives and
libraries. Because they worked from sketchy notations, it was
difficult to translate them into actual movements. From the
outset, the group indulged in creative reconstruction, devis-
ing their own style in the process. Once the basic Seven
Champions' style had solidified, they branched out into
adapting other dances and composing new dances to broaden
their repertoire. By 1983 they had given their first workshop
in Molly dancing. They taught the collected material rather

than their own repertoire. Later in the day they held a competition among the participants to create a dance based on
the notation of a collected dance. This was an influential
exercise. The Champions believe a group of Molly dancers
must be able to develop their own dances. The hope was to
foster interest and enthusiasm while encouraging originality
rather than blind imitation. The Seven Champions paved the
way for experimentation and creativity within the Molly
dance genre. The gradual increase in innovative teams is a
direct result of their influence.

The majority of contemporary Molly dancers have some
first hand knowledge of the music and choreography of the
collected dances. A few groups however, have developed their
styles without recourse or reference to this pre-revival repertoire. They represent a second generation of Molly dancers
whose performances are based on the compositions and style
of other living performers (often, the Seven Champions are
the model for these groups). This generation of Molly dancers
has taken the form further away from the source. Their dance
style and repertoire have spread well beyond southern
England.[18]

Handsome Molly[19] is one example of how the genre has
travelled from its East Anglian roots. The group was formed
in 1993 by members of other display dance groups in the
Princeton area in the United States. They became interested
in Molly dancing after seeing the Marlborough Morris
Women perform their interpretation of a Molly dance. Later,
they viewed a video tape of the Seven Champions and were
inspired to form their own group . They had very little information to go on other than articles published in *English Dance
and Song* and the video tape mentioned above. Handsome
Molly's first dance was a version of the Seven Champion's
dance 'Inertia Reel' (learned from the video tape) and most of
their subsequent dances have been made up or adapted from
social dances (including an American square dance). Over
time they learned two dances from the traditional repertoire,
so they would have some dances in common with other Molly
teams. They usually dance to a solo singer in imitation of the
Seven Champions. Their dances are formally taught and
their style is similar to the Champions', though faster. The
group performs all year and observes Plough Monday with a
special tour (including a plough). Their costume varies

Dave Roe (Molly) of the Seven Champions glaring at the audience, September 1994. *Photo: Elaine Bradtke* depending on whether they are appearing with another group with whom they share dancers. When they are on their own, they wear predominantly black clothes, caps or berets, and hard soled shoes. They wear black face, combined with other colours or sometimes partial masks.[20] The flamboyantly dressed man/woman in a flowered hat and flounced skirt stands out against the tough, dark appearance of the others. The leader of the group, a woman, dances as the lord at the top of the set in top hat and a tailcoat.

As more Molly groups form and more dances are composed there may eventually emerge a more clearly defined style. Even now, the influence of the Seven Champions may be seen among the innovative teams. Either directly, as in including a Seven Champions dance in the repertoire, or indirectly, in imitation of choreographic elements. Though many Molly groups perform at least one of the pre-revival dances, as time goes by there will likely be more groups who only know newly composed dances. It is unlikely that there will emerge a standard repertoire beyond the pre-revival dances, despite the use of video tape as a learning tool. Innovative Molly dancers, by definition, prefer to differ from the status quo.

What changed and what remained the same?
The dance and music
Some of the elements which have carried over from the performance pre-revival Molly dancing; the double column set, the position of the musician, the frequent use of hornpipe tunes, the typical AABB structure of both music and dance. These are defining elements of the genre. The exceptions to these standard elements are striking because they were devised by the innovative dancers to give their dance a new look to appeal to the masses. In innovating, there seem to be certain elements of performance which are more open to change than others. The variety and number of instruments has increased to include electric violins, the human voice and even a Romanian wooden saxophone called a 'taragot'. The inclusion of female dancers, and the development of dances for uneven or small numbers of performers are related to the demographics of the Molly dancers themselves. The emphasis now is more on performance for the sake of performance, with greater attention being paid to details such as coordinat-

The Seven Champions performing a 'Tiller Girls' figure

Photo: Elaine Bradtke

ed movements and varied choreography. There is a broad
range of source material from which the innovative dancers
draw their music and choreography. Popular music, social
dances from foreign countries or theatrical genres are all fair
game. They further colour their creative work by 'mollyising'
the elements they have borrowed from other genres, so that
they blend in with the more traditional elements. The innovative groups have changed the performance of Molly dancing
by using new materials in old patterns, and old material with
new embellishments.

Events and venues

Molly dancers, once only seen in East Anglian villages and
market towns, have materialised in cities, suburbs and even
foreign countries. What had been solely a seasonal street
entertainment may now be seen any time of the year at festivals and in auditoria. Molly dancers used to perform as a
means of supplementing their income during times of little
work. Now, members of the middle class use their spare time
and money to participate in Molly dancing as a hobby.
Though they are less disreputable than in the past, they are
also less dependent on the largesse of individual spectators,
preferring in many cases to omit the traditional cadging altogether. Instead many innovative groups earn their expense
money as hired performers, appearing before knowledgeable
audiences. The increase in the number and variety of venues,
and changes in the composition of the audience has effected
the entire genre. Innovative groups, especially the Seven
Champions, have adapted their act to suit the stages and
sophisticated audiences found in festivals. It is ironic that
contemporary dancers, such as the Seven Champions, give
more of an exhibition and pay more attention to the amuse-
ment of their audience, yet demand less in direct repayment
than the pre-revival dancers did.

The majority of Molly dancers today have abandoned
strict historical reconstructions. They allude to the origins of
the dances, while performing them in a very up-to-date setting. Or they may use newly composed dances in a traditional
village setting. The innovative dance groups have taken a
midwinter, high-spirited request for largesse and turned it
into a season-less form of entertainment. The amount of
attention contemporary Molly dancers pay to their audience

is a direct result of their concern with mass appeal. Innovative Molly dancers such as the Seven Champions are happy to reinvent the tradition in order to appeal to the tastes of their audience. They are repaid in kind by the applause and enthusiasm that greets their efforts.

Cultural context

The status of the individuals who perform Molly dances has improved since the pre-revival days. They are members of the middle class and thus enjoy a higher station in life than their predecessors. As Molly dancers, however, they do not have a high status within the folk revival community and as folk dance enthusiasts, they do not have a very high status outside of it. The musician has become more integral to the group, and is no longer a hired outsider. They lead something of a double life due to their participation in traditional pursuits of farm labourers, even as their comfortable way of life allows them the leisure time for such activities. The shift from agricultural workers to white-collar workers has brought with it some of the organisational strategies and hierarchy associated with middle-class norms. Many groups are formally structured, and their members may undergo special training before they dance in public. The improved status of the dancers and change in cultural context is related to the alteration in the implicit function of the dance. The Molly dancers of today do not dance to assert their importance in the village economy, to settle old disputes or to raise much needed cash. They dance in order to breathe new life into an old dance form, and to vent their creative impulses. In doing so within the folk community they express their dissatisfaction with commercial and political efforts to create a homogeneous society.

Though in a state of decline, the itinerant performances by Molly dancers persisted into the early twentieth century. These dancers relied on the simple disguise of cross-dressing and blackened faces for anonymity. They used the feast dances and music of the common people for their repertoire. And they depended on the continuing benevolence of their neighbours in exchange for their performance. The Molly dancers danced out of economic need and as an occasionally destructive reminder that the economy of the region depended on their labour. As disreputable as it had become in the

nineteenth century, it took twentieth century farming techniques, the devastation of two world wars, and the growth of
the welfare state to bring an end to Molly dancing. By this
point, the English folk revival had been active for quite some
time, but the contemptible reputation of the Molly dancers
and the prosaic, simple choreography of their dances caused
the collectors to pass them by.

Although there had been limited success in the 1970s at
reviving Molly dances by the Cambridge Morris Men and
Mepal Molly, the genre, as they performed it, remained
obscure within the larger revival. Once the Seven Champions
began to reinvent Molly dancing however, interest in these
dances grew. Gradually the performance of so called Molly
dances began to increase in popularity. Some groups were traditionalist in interpretation and repertoire, others were more
adventurous and emulated the Seven Champions by performing invented or adapted dances in a flamboyant style.
Many groups fall somewhere in between the two extremes,
but they all, to a greater or lesser extent, use creative re-inter-
pretation of the past through the present. The reinvention of
Molly dancing and other dormant genres was an expression
of a desire for a display dance form that suites the tastes and
interests of the late twentieth century performers and
audience.

For the performers, there is no longer an economic basis
for their performance. In fact, as is the case with most amateurs, Molly dancers spend time and money in order to take
part in something they enjoy. Satisfaction is gained through
participation within a community of like-minded individuals. The folk revival itself serves as a method for many to cope
with and escape from the alienation, the loss of self and community in the urban, industrialised, mass-produced,
homogenised society which permeates their everyday life. As
Peter Narváez writes:

> Folk revival arises out of a restless or vehement
> dissatisfaction with one's own contemporary cul-
> ture. Unlike other social movements that dwell on
> the creation of altogether new alternatives (e.g.,
> futuristic utopianism) folk revivalists are inclined
> to search for viable cultural alternatives in folk
> cultures of the past, oftentimes folk cultures that
> are conceived as being in some way connected to

their own history.[21]

The Molly dance genre has allowed a freedom of expression formerly unavailable to the display dancer. Molly dancers nowadays are encouraged or even expected to create their own dances, style, techniques, and musical accompaniment. This gives them a sense of ownership that does not come with learning dances collected from some distant village a hundred years ago. Instead it is a dance from their own region, reworked for modern performance, or indeed something they devised themselves. It is this combination of being connected to the past yet not closely constrained by it which is at the centre of the growing interest in Molly dancing. Perhaps this represents the future of English display dance, another step beyond preservation into the realm of creativity. Only time will tell.

Notes

1. Stephen, Nissenbaum, *The Battle for Christmas*, (New York: Knopf, 1996), p. 8.
2. The south Midlands region is described by Keith Chandler in 'Morris Dancing in the South Midlands: The Socio-cultural Background to 1914,' *Traditional Dance*, 2 (1983) 58–90, p.59. as being an area roughly within a thirty-five mile radius of Witney, Oxfordshire. This is where the majority of revived Cotswold-style dances were collected. Dances from this region are often referred to as Cotswold morris to distinguish them from the Welsh border dances, and the North-west processional dances. Although south Midlands is more geographically accurate, I will continue to use the term Cotswold in the manner of the dancers themselves.
3. George Frampton, 'A Penny for the Ploughboys ...,' *The Morris Dancer* 2:8 (1989), p. 122.
4. *Ibid*.
5. George Frampton, 'The Ramsey Molly Dancers, Straw Bears and Plough Monday,' *The Morris Dancer* 2:6 (1988), p. 90.
6. Display dances are meant to be watched as opposed to the social dances, which are participatory.
7. Cecil J. Sharp, *The Country Dance Book Part I: Containing a Description of Eighteen Traditional Dances Collected in Country Villages*, 2nd ed (London: Novello and Company, 1934; reprint ed Carlshalton, Surrey: H. Styles, 1985), p. 12.
8. *Ibid*.
9. A reel is a weaving figure commonly found in English dances.
10. A recording of music and text related to Welsh Border Morris and Molly dancing published by Island Records.
11. Frampton, 'Penny for the Ploughboys ...,' p. 146–7.
12. Rob Elliott, *Don't Blame Me, I'm Only the Triangle Player* (Worcester; Worcs: Square one Publications, 1991), p.1.
13. Team is a term used by the dancers themselves to designate a group. It does not, however imply competition between dance teams. The term 'side' has the same

meaning in this context.

14. Dave Dye, Interviewed by Elaine Bradtke 4 Sept. 1994, Eastbourne, England.
15. There is one dance in the pre-revival repertoire which calls for handkerchiefs to be tied, or linked together between partners. This is quite different from the Cotswold style of using handkerchiefs as an extension of the hand movements.
16. Dave Dye,1994.
17. Russell Wortley and Cyril Papworth, 'Molly Dancing in South-West Cambridgeshire,' *English Dance and Song* 40 (1978) pp. 58–9.
18. In the summer of 1996 the Country Dance and Song Society (USA) included classes in Molly dancing at two of their week long dance camps. These classes were taught by members of two different second generation groups. Both teachers have to a greater or lesser extent, based their interpretation of Molly dancing on what they have seen of the Seven Champions. At least one North American group has begun to perform Molly dances as a direct result of these workshops.
19. Their name comes from an Anglo-American folk song. They have localised the tradition by using folk songs with regional references to accompany their dances.
20. They abandoned the idea of strict black face because they found the American public reacted negatively.
21. Peter Narváez, 'Paradoxical Aesthetics of the Blues Revival,' in *Transforming Tradition: Folk Music Revivals Examined*. Neil V. Rosenberg, ed. (Urbana and Chicago: University of Illinois Press, 1993), p. 244

Further reading

Bradtke, Elaine. 1997. 'Molly Dancing and the Seven Champions: Postmodernism and the Re-invention of Tradition,' PhD. Diss., University of Maryland Baltimore County. UMI microform

Bradtke, Elaine. 1999. *Truculent Rustics: Molly dancing in East Anglia before 1940*. London: Folklore Society.

Dommett, Roy. 1986. *Roy Dommett's Morris Notes*. Anthony G. Barrand ed., 2nd ed., [n.p]: Country Dance and Song Society.

Frampton, George. 1987. 'Anecdotes from the Molly Dancers,' *The Morris Dancer* 2(5):pp. 78–9.

– 1988. 'The Ramsey Molly Dancers, Straw Bears and Plough Monday,' *The Morris Dancer* 2(6):pp. 89–91.

– 1989. 'A Penny for the Ploughboys ... ', *The Morris Dancer* 2(8):pp. 121–4.

– 1993. *Pity the Poor Ploughboy – Balsham's Plough Monday*. Tonbridge, Kent: self-published.

– 1996. *Vagrants, Rogues and Vagabonds: Plough Monday Tradition in Old Huntingdonshire and the Soke of Peterborogh*. Tonbridge, Kent: self-published.

Hulme, Ann-Marie and Peter Clifton. 1978. 'Social Dancing

in a Norfolk Village 1900-1945,' *Folk Music Journal* 3 (4): pp. 359–77.

Hutton, Ronald. 1994. *The Rise and Fall of Merry England: The Ritual Year 1400–1700*. Oxford: Oxford University Press.

Needham, Joseph and Arthur L. Peck. 1933. 'Molly Dancing in East Anglia,' *Journal of the English Folk Dance & Song Society* 1(2): pp. 79–85.

Palmer, William. 1974. 'Plough Monday 1933 at Little Downham,' *English Dance and Song* 36(1): pp. 24–5

Papworth, Cyril. 1974. 'The Comberton Broom Dance,' *English Dance & Song* 36(1): p. 30.

Porter, Enid. 1969. *Cambridgeshire Customs and Folklore*. London: Routledge Kegan Paul

– 1974. *The Folklore of East Anglia*. London: Batsford; Totowa, New Jersey: Rowman & Littlefield.

Sharp, Cecil J. 1934. *The Country Dance Book Part I: Containing a Description of Eighteen Traditional Dances Collected in Country Villages*. 2nd ed, London: Novello and Company; reprint ed Carlshalton, Surrey: H. Styles, 1985.

Thompson, E.P. 1991. *Customs in Common*. London: Merlin; New York: The New Press.

Underdown, David. 1985. *Revel, Riot, and Rebellion: Popular Politics and Culture in England 1603–1660*. Oxford: Clarendon Press.

Wortley, Russell and Cyril Papworth. 1978. 'Molly Dancing in South-West Cambridgeshire,' *English Dance and Song* 40: pp. 58–9.

Eva Johnson and partner, music hall postcard showing a
Dutch character clog dance, n.d. *Author's collection*

The Ladies' Clog Dancing Contest of 1898[1]

Caroline Radcliffe

Few people today have any idea how a Lancashire clog dance is performed. For most, the mention of a clog dance summons up the image of a character dressed in Dutch national costume, with huge carved-out wooden clogs dancing clomping steps at the local boy scout and girl guide gangshow. Others – those perhaps with a moderate awareness of British traditional dance – might picture a beer-swilling morris team performing simple, heavy steps in front of the village pub. Both of these images are far from the intricate, fast, light and highly-skilled steps of the nineteenth century form of clog dancing that came to be termed as 'Lancashire'.

There has been little serious research on clog dancing so I have looked at a competition that took place in London at the end of the nineteenth century and hope to show how the figures of the female clog dancer and the juvenile clog dancer eventually coalesced to leave us with today's impression of the little Dutch dancer.

Although clog dancing must have evolved alongside the use of wooden soled shoes, the style known as 'Lancashire' can be traced back to the Industrial Revolution. R.U. Sayce dates both the wooden soled patten and the clog back to the Middle Ages, and even though there were many regional variations of style and clog types, an association with the area of Lancashire dating as far back as the fourteenth century is often cited.[2] By the second half of the nineteenth century the clogs used for stagedancing were a Lancashire-style, wooden-soled, leather shoe with laces. By then, most of the steps used on stage originated from Lancashire.

Playbills demonstrate that clog dancing occurred on the legitimate stage as an extension of the stage hornpipe, a performance platform in which professional actors or dancers could demonstrate virtuosity, prowess or trick or comic steps, incorporated into the main play, a pantomime, or dividing the programme.[3] The mixed bill format of programming was designed to appeal to lower-class audiences and the inclusion of the clog dance must have been a response to the rising predominance of the industrial worker. The increasing improbability of the trick feats of hornpipes and clog dances played on the audiences taste for both rivalry and suspense. With the passing of the 1843 Theatre Act, the legitimate theatre sought to distinguish itself from saloon entertainments, seeking a higher class-specific audience, omitting elements which would attract lower-class patrons or incite disruptive behaviour. Although clog dancing persisted into the second half of the century in the provincial theatres, it now found its metier in the developing music hall. By the second half of the nineteenth century, clog dancing was a staple and popular act in the provincial and the London music hall. But it was still mainly confined to the almost ghettoised territory of the lower-class halls.

It is suggested that Lancashire clog dancing originated in the cotton mills as the operatives stepped in their clogs in time to the rhythms of the power looms. Certainly surviving steps and dances indicate an industrial influence. Pat Tracey[4] points to steps common to all dances with names such as the pick, the shuttle, the two up and two down, derived from weaving processes or components of the looms and imitative of both their actions and sounds;[5] the steps of Bill Gibbons,[6] a bargeman on the Leeds-Liverpool canal, imitated the sounds of the barge engine. There would also seem to be a considerable Irish influence with many clog dancers of Irish descent or parentage. Steps are common to Irish and Lancashire step dancing and many of the tunes used for the Lancashire clog dance are Irish. This cross-cultural fertilisation was due to the large proportion of immigrant workers in Lancashire. Almost without exception, clog dancers appear to originate from industrial occupations, immigrant or travelling communities, or families of performers. Each of these developing factors appear throughout the 1898 Ladies' Clog Dancing Contest and account for the often ambiguous reports on the contest.

The majority of historical references to clog dancing refer to the male dancer. The Ladies' Contest is unusual in that it refers specifically to women and children and that it took place in a major, higher-class London music hall. The Ladies' Clog Dancing Contest for the 'Championship of the World' commenced on Monday 25 April, 1898 at the Washington Music Hall in Battersea, London. After six days of heats, the finals culminated with the presentation to the winner of a handsome gold jewelled shield, £10 in prize money and the prized title of Champion.

The Ladies' Contest was promoted by Mr. J.H. Wood, a music hall manager who, in 1880, had initiated a championship at the Princess's Palace in Leeds in which Dan Leno, the then little-known music hall performer, was pitted against some of Britain's most famous dancers. After a series of fiercely disputed contests, Leno eventually secured the title of Champion of the World, going on to become Britain's best-loved male music hall and pantomime performer.[7] Having moved to London to manage the Peoples' Empire music hall in Bow, Wood had, in February 1898, revived the male clog Championship of the World.[8] It was the publicity surrounding this revival of the Championship that inspired a series of letters in the music hall press from various stage clog dancers leading to the instigation of the Ladies' Championship.

The ensuing interest in clog dancing in the professional stage press prompted Miss Nellie Martell 'Warranted Three Star, the Popular London Comedienne and Burlesque Artist' to issue 'A Challenge to the World', placing the following advertisement in the back pages of the *Era*:

> Hearing so much about the Clog Dancing abilities of certain American Ladies now Appearing in the British Isles Miss Martell wishes to state that she will Dance any One of them or any Lady in the World, in Clogs for not less than £50 a-side, such Contest to take part in London; or she will Dance in America for not less than £100 a-side, and Expenses. £5 is deposited with Mr Tom Shaw, 86, Strand, and anyone placing in his hands a like

The Ladies' Clog Dancing Contest, from *Variety*, 23 April 1898. *By permission of the British Library*

sum will ensure a Match, and remember no one is barred.

Miss Martell has not Danced in Clogs Publicly for the last Seven years, and does not intend to, unless this challenge is accepted.

The above is no Yankee bluff, but an honest British Challenge, backed up by British Gold.

Miss Nellie Martell, the Champion Lady Clog-Dancer of the World Agent, Tom Shaw, 86, Strand, London.[9]

Like most music hall performers, Martell was employed at three London music halls at the time of her advertisement – the Metropolitan, Gatti's and the Temple of Varieties, travelling from one to the other every evening except Sundays. According to her own publicity, her comic song was going down well, making audiences 'smile, titter and grin';[10] but the reviewer for the *Era* also singled out her impressive step dancing.

Miss Nellie Martell made us sad on the night of our visit by telling us that 'Mary's lost her reputation all through a sailor with a ginger nob', but she cheered us up soon afterwards by some very finely executed steps. Miss Martell, we understand, claims championship honours as a lady clog dancer, and she should be hard to beat.[11]

The following week Nellie Coleman, described in her publicity as 'Little Nellie Coleman of Venny & Coleman, late of the Sisters Coleman, & a sister to Johnny Coleman (now in Australia), one of our greatest Dancers', accepted Nellie Martell's challenge ...

... but for £20 a-side, as £50 is out of the question. I will dance her any style she pleases. As the world is wide and I don't know everybody in it, I consider myself one of England's Greatest Lady Step Dancers. I have not won for myself Title of Champion but hope to do so. Now astonishing the Public at the Grand Theatre, Newcastle. I am not a Dark Horse. Dancers who understand Dancing acknowledge I know how to use my feet ...[12]

Miss Nellie Martell, *Era*, 7 July 1898.
By permission of the British Library. BL: LD73

Martell was not prepared to lower her stakes for Coleman, instead accepting a response from Ada Dell, issued the following week. Dell was currently playing principal boy in Aladdin at the Theatre Royal, Bristol. Like Martell she was a comic singer and dancer who was appreciatively described in reviews. Not only were her singing and fine step dancing singled out, but also her acting, a 'charming presence' and a 'delightful figure'. In the cavern scene Dell (still in her role as Aladdin) managed to introduce a 'Safety Pin' song, an allusion to the Bristol Rugby Club and a 'coon' song with accompanying step dance.[13]

Whilst accepting Martell's challenge, Dell also deposited £5 with the *Era*, opening a Ladies' Sweepstake competition, to dance three dances: Step (Scottische Time), American Buck, and Clog Dance. The winner would take the pool, donating half of the winnings to the Music Hall Benevolent Fund.[14] Wood immediately recognised an opportunity to promote another clog contest, issuing a list of rules in the *Era* the following week .

1. Each Competitor to Dance in Clogs without any fittings or Jingles attached.[15]
2. Two competitors to Dance Each Evening, which will be Drawn for and Published in the Era Two Weeks before the Contest.
3. Each Competitor to Dance Twelve steps and a Shuffle-Off (to Shuffle off the Toe).
4. The one who gets the Most Marks on the Decision of the Judges and Referee for Time, Carriage, Execution and Original Steps, to be proclaimed Champion Lady Clog Dancer of the World ...[16]

The contest was originally planned to take place in Easter week, but in the event took place two weeks later. By April, fourteen lady contestants (including two children) had entered the competition. In the meantime a separate match was also scheduled for May between Ada Dell and Nellie Martell.

The correspondence leading up to the contest demonstrates a number of factors common to clog dancing in the Victorian and Edwardian music hall. Wood's publicity for his great Championship revivals gives the impression that the championship contest was an isolated event in the music hall. But for as long as the music hall had existed, clog dancing contests had featured as an entertainment item. Clog dancing was certainly not confined to the stage – steps had been created and transmitted through generations of families and pupils to create an orally transmitted tradition of dance, performed throughout homes, dancing schools, pubs, fairs and community celebrations. But throughout the nineteenth century, clog dancing evolved as a competitive dance form and by 1850 'every village had its champion clog dancer'.[17] By the 1870s, clog dancing was at the height of its popularity, becoming a regular music hall feature. Retaining its popularity throughout the 1880s, it lost its prominence as an entertainment item in the 90s, giving way to different variety acts.

The *Era*'s correspondence demonstrates that clog dancing was not an exclusively male domain and that both men and women competed for championship titles throughout the country. Although most documentation on clog dancing refers to male performers, the Ladies' Contest of 1898 highlights the number of female clog dancers who performed professionally, differing little from their male colleagues in their professional approach.[18] The challenges issued by Martell, Dell and Coleman are consistent with the style of publicity used in general by stage clog dancers. Martell's initial advert demonstrates the role of the challenging bravado employed in order to attract good competition. It also demonstrates the high stakes involved in a match. A good music hall wage averaged between £2 and £10 a week – the winner of a clog match could considerably raise his or her income by implementing high stakes and receiving large winnings and prize money. The winner would also be offered well-paid music hall bookings by proprietors keen to secure a new champion. The clog match was essentially a vehicle for betting and the Ladies' Contest remained as such – irrespective of its association with women. It was the involvement of money and the excitement of placing a bet that gave the edge to an art form that was otherwise frequently described in terms such as 'a merely mechanical exercise'.[19]

Martell's advert also alludes to the fiercely nationalistic or regional nature of the clog competition. Like gambling, this was another element that drew the audience into rival factions, inciting a more exciting competition. The match tran-

scended the individual performers to become more about
rival nationalities or regional affiliations. The competitors of
the Ladies' Contest were described by name and by where
they were based: Ettie Godwin, Lily Gaston, Lily Chard,
Lilian Rigby, Connie Chard, Bertha Winder and Ada Dell
were all based in London; Minnie Ray from Manchester, Eva
Reed – Liverpool, Cissy Sullivan – Stockton-on-Tees but representing Ireland, Ethel Stanley – Newcastle, Annie
Liscombe – South Shields, and Bella Perman – Australia.[20]
The winner's home-town was also announced at the final:
'Manchester in the form of Miss Ray carried off the Shield ...
Miss Liscombe from South Shields came in for an
easy 2nd ...'[21]

My research has shown that many stage clog dancers originated from Lancashire, north-east England or Ireland.
These are still the main areas in Britain for hard shoe and
clog dancing. Throughout the nineteenth century there was
much movement between Ireland and Lancashire and many
performers eventually settled in America or Australia. The
descriptions of the entrants for the Ladies' Contest corrobo-
rates this research.

Many of the dancers were from clog dancing families and
had been learning since they were children. Minnie Ray, the
twenty-five year old winner of the Ladies' Contest, was the
daughter of a famous champion, Ben Ray, who had been one
of the original judges in the great contest of 1880 in which
Dan Leno had competed.[22] She had started dancing at the age
of seven, learning from her father. She formed a clog duo with
her sister, which broke up when her sister married. She then
developed a solo music hall act in which her clog dancing featured. Bella Perman, aged twenty-five from Sydney, Australia,
had entered the contest but was forced to withdraw by the
music hall manager Sir Oswald Stoll, who would not release
her from a music hall booking. She therefore issued her own
challenge to dance the winner of the contest which Minnie
Ray took up and won.[23] Perman had commenced her career at
the age of twelve with her brothers Percy and Willie as part of
The Perman Family. She came to England in 1896 as one of
The Perman Trio with whom she was performing at the time
of the contest. Cissie Sullivan, who came third in the Ladies'
Contest, was the daughter of a celebrated champion clog
dancer, Mike Sullivan. Two of the competitors, Lilian Rigby

and Bertha Winder were just eight years old. Lilian Rigby competed and was awarded a special gold medal for 'her pluck in entering the championship contest, being the youngest competitor',[24] but although Bertha Winder had danced during the organised heats she had not been allowed to enter the competition. Wood stated that had Bertha Winder competed there would have been 'little doubt of her being champion dancer, not excepting the very best of our present day performers' – having 'paralysed' the audience by her performance. She was also presented with an extra prize.[25] The involvement of two talented children in the competition added an extra attraction for the audience and Wood's preferential treatment of them clearly acted as a good public relations exercise.

Child dancers were extremely skilled, having been disciplined from the moment they could wear clogs, and they were generally exploited on the stage at the earliest opportunity. Charlie Chaplin records joining the child clog dancing troupe the Eight Lancashire Lads in 1898, at the age of nine.[26] It was run by a Lancashire man, William Jackson, who had learnt clog dancing in Liverpool. Two of Jackson's own children were members of the troupe, one of whom (according to Chaplin) was his nine year old daughter dressed up as a boy. Chaplin's description of his time with the Eight Lancashire Lads along with his biographer David Robinson's research (including lists of the troupe's tours) gives details as to the conditions and training of a child dancer. Chaplin trained for six weeks before he was eligible to dance on stage but it was many more weeks before he was able to perform a solo dance. According to Chaplin, the 'lads' wore the traditional clog dancing costume of white linen blouse, a lace collar, plush knickerbocker trousers and red dancing shoes. They did not wear makeup but were encouraged to keep smiling at the audience. A review quoted by Robinson indicates that apart from their traditional dances, the troupe also incorporated character dances – they were described as looking picturesque in their 'charming continental costumes'.[27] They were also employed in pantomime. Chaplin toured with the Eight Lancashire Lads throughout 1899 and 1900 but the troupe continued well into the 1900s. Chaplin was well looked after with board and lodging provided and his mother was paid half a crown a week. An account book from the

Glasgow Empire music hall shows that by February 1901 Jackson was being paid £20 for a week's performances by the Eight Lancashire Lads, 'vocalists and clog dancers'.[28]

Other child clog dancers were disciplined by their parents or by professional trainers in the same way that a wrestler or footballer might be trained, having been 'talent-spotted'.[29] As a professional troupe, the Eight Lancashire Lads' welfare was answerable to the local county court and Jackson was compelled to enroll them at local schools and to comply with certain licensing restrictions applicable for the employment of juveniles in music halls – child dancers trained at home had none of these restrictions placed upon them.

The music hall clog act at this time tended to be a straight-forward display of skill based around a competition or on honours already obtained in the form of a championship title or belt. Great importance was placed on the public display of the championship cup, or the belt and medals which are still worn today.[30]

The clog dance was also included as a standard part of a black-face minstrel act often known as a 'coon' dance or 'plantation' dance, such as the one performed by Ada Dell in Aladdin. These originated in America and can be regarded as a different genre to the Lancashire-based style of competitive dancing performed out of character. The standard competition and performance costume (as described by Chaplin) consisted of knee breeches and a loose shirt, often with various decorative items such as a small waistcoat, sashes and ribbons, fancy collars or a cap to denote the competitors' 'colours'.[31] The women in the Ladies' Contest were no exception to this rule, displaying a variety of colours and trimmings but retaining the basic knee breeches and shirt. The photograph of the competitors published in *Variety* the week before the competition shows some of the contestants in costume, issuing a description of their chosen 'colours' in the same way that a jockey for a horse race might be described.

> Miss Minnie Ray, purple body with gold braid, scarlet sleeves, black velvet cap with gold fringe, and white knee breeches; Miss Annie Liscombe, black satin bodice, pale blue knee breeches, and Union Jack sash; Miss Cissy Sullivan, pink and green; Miss Ettic Goodwin (sic), red knee breeches, with red sash and cap and white blouse; Miss

Miss Minnie Ray, the winner of the Ladies' Clog Dancing
Contest of 1898, from *Era*, 21 May 1898.

By permission of the British Library. BL: LD73

Ada Dell, orange and black; Miss Connie Chard,
black velvet breeches, white blouse, and red sash;
Miss Lily Chard, black velvet breeches, white
blouse and yellow sash; Miss Lily Hum, red, white
and blue; Miss Lilian Rigby, ruby zouave and blue
sash, with black stockings; Miss Edith Stanley, red
breeches, white blouse, and blue stockings and
sash; Miss Bertha Winder, red, white and gold;
and Miss Lillie Gaston, heliotrope.[32]

The ladies' costumes were essentially the same as the standard male costume with their two main features, the traditional breeches and the colours denoting the individual
competitors. The breeches were essential in allowing the
intricate clog steps, the movement of which nearly all origi-
nates from below the knee, to be viewed clearly by audience
and judges. The performers' colours enhanced the sporting
nature of clog dancing and facilitated the bets placed on the
individuals.

In all the aspects discussed so far, the format of the Ladies'
Contest differed little from the men's, although the rules had
been tightened and improved in light of irregularities that
had occurred in the men's competition. The women were
required to dance only twelve steps (each 'step' actually being
a unit of eight bars duration, made up of many steps) as
opposed to the twenty steps danced by the men; the womens'
prizes were correspondingly lower than the mens' – George
Burns, the male champion, had won a championship belt
plus £20 in prize money whereas Minnie Ray was awarded a
jewelled shield and £10.10 shillings.

The noteworthy difference between the womens' and the
men's contests is not the nature of the contest itself but how
the events were reported. The men's contest is always
described briefly and factually with no reference to the competitors' physical appearance, but when the women are
referred to, the commentators continually apply physical
criticisms with references to their figures, dress and 'feminine' accoutrements in the form of sashes, collars and
ribbons.

The *Era*'s commentator was no exception; whilst reporting
the private match between Ada Dell and Nellie Martell he
incongruously mixes physical allusions with detailed techni-
cal description.

Miss Ada Dell, *Era*, 21 May 1898.
By permission of the British Library. BL: LD73

The first of the ladies to tap the raised platform
with her clogs was Miss Ada Dell, a bright, pleas-
ing brunette, of whom Bristolians have very pleasant recollections in pantomime at the Theatre
Royal, in the city of the west. Miss Dell, who wore
a maize-coloured blouse trimmed with black lace
and black satin, soon got into her stride, and
did her allotted task with considerable neatness,
but with a certain amount of stiffness. Miss Nellie
Martell, whose form was admirably set off by
a patriotic Union Jack blouse and blue tights,
commenced somewhat nervously, but rapidly
gaining confidence put a great deal of varied
work into her steps, indulging in heeltaps and
showing generally greater freedom of style than
her predecessor ...[33]

Although we have seen that the womens' costumes were
essentially traditional and similar to the men's, when asked to
comment on the ladies' championship contest, Wood's first
observation was 'Let me see. Some of the ladies will wear very
costly dresses'. Wood could not help applying accepted
Victorian stereotypes – a woman was viewed as an ornament
on which to hang costly and decorative clothes and the theatrical convention was to describe the actress not only in
terms of her performance but by what she was wearing. Wood
was unprepared to allow the incompatibility of the traditional knee breeches and competitive personality of the clog
dancer to undermine the accepted female theatrical stereotype. Tracy C. Davis discusses the paradox of the Victorian
actress that Wood found impossible to ignore:

A series of paradoxes characterizes actresses'
appearance on stage: while embodying the ideals
of feminine beauty and setting the standards for
female fashion, they were 'defeminized' by the
very act of taking up a public career in the theatre.
The same women who impersonated Dianas and
Vestias also claimed a place in a competitive co-
sexual world of work, spent their evenings away
from home, and exhibited themselves in the public gaze. To complicate matters, femininity was
the quality traditionally credited with making

women the objects of male desire, yet actresses'
'defeminization' made them more desirable than
ever in a sexual sense. On stage, femininity and
desirability co-existed, yet in order to accept the
fiction of an idealized femininity in a stage per-
sona, Victorians were required to separate the
defeminized actress from her roles. They then had
to decide which part of the individual would
receive moral strictures.[34]

Wood wished to describe the female clog dancer through the
terminology usually applied to the Victorian actress in terms
of physical beauty and decorative appeal. He did not want to
undermine this convention by describing the female clog
dancers in the same terms as the male. He also recognised
that the association of stage dancing – and particularly clog
dancing – was incompatible with a respectable feminine per-
sona, and sought to compensate for this through the glam-
ourisation of the women, setting them up as objects of sexual
desire.

The combination of the women's career in the music hall,
in which they danced publicly – displaying their figures and
their legs – was historically a dangerous one. The music hall
had always come under moral reproof – associated with prostitution and alcohol – and stage dancing had always been
viewed as a flagrant incitement to sexual lust. J.S. Bratton
outlines the provocative role of the tight white breeches of the
midshipman 'revealing the outline of buttock and thigh'
worn by female hornpipe dancers throughout the nineteenth
century. As a female dance the hornpipe's 'encoded meanings
included those of sensual and sexual display'.[35] The paradigm
of the cross-dressed female also added an element of sexual
ambiguity that heightened the mystique of the female performer. By the late nineteenth century the 'championship
hornpipe' was the main competition dance although it had by
then lost its exclusive association with the sailor.

Clog dancing had links with gambling and was rooted in
the industrial working class – associations which the increasingly class conscious London music hall was eager to detach
itself from. The theatrical press described the betting on the
ladies in euphemistic terms, playing down its centrality to the
match, although it could not be ignored entirely.

> Already speculation as to the result is decidedly
> brisk, among the most fancied ladies being Ada
> Dell, Cissy Sullivan ... [36]

The wearing of the clog itself came to typify the labouring classes and by the end of the nineteenth century the clog was increasingly banned from public places.[37] Many of the steps originated from the sounds of industrial machinery used in the cotton mills, barges and coal mines. Many people were uneasy about a skill that arose from the working-class, and although stage dancing was usually the exception to the rule, the display of women clog dancing was often deemed unsuitable. The oral recollections of a present day clog dancer, Pat Tracey, confirms these views. Tracey's family's clog steps can be traced back to her grandfather who was born in east Lancashire in 1856 and some steps may originate as far back as the 1820s.[38] When asked whether women ever danced in the cotton factories of east Lancashire, Tracey replied:

> Yes they did, but they weren't allowed to dance in
> public in the part of the world I come from ... I
> won't say ever, but it was considered a little bit of
> a disgrace for a woman to be seen clog dancing in
> public ... It was a man's dance, I think basically.[39]

But from other accounts, particularly from the research carried out by the Instep team based in Newcastle, it would seem that many women did dance in public, not only as stage dancers but in local contests often arranged around public holidays and fairs, or simply in a local 'go-as-you-please', a spontaneous demonstration or contest of singing or dancing taking place in a pub.[40] Often these women were from travelling or immigrant families and were perhaps already viewed as outsiders. Certainly, from all accounts, the woman who clog danced displaced herself from the status quo and deliberately attracted the attention that most Victorian women were encouraged to avoid. Clog dancing posed a cultural threat to the middle classes. A low art form which appeared to be authentically working-class, grounded in the industrial vernacular, played on the earlier fears of a labour uprising necessitating a repression of a working-class identity which could possibly lead to subversion. This combined with the sexually charged, immoral stereotype of the female dancer produced a female image that completely subverted middle-class Victorian ideology.

Arnold Bennett demonstrates both class fear and gyno-phobia in his fictional account of a female clog dancer, Miss Florence Simcox, in his novel *Clayhanger*.[41] The passage is also interesting for its inclusion of many of the elements of clog dancing already discussed. The year is 1872, Florence is the wife of a Mr Offlow, a Lancashire comic with sporting connections. As the champion female clog dancer of the mid-lands she is touring 'the realms of her championship ... min-gling terriers, recitations and clogs'. The scene described is set in a 'free and easy' or 'go-as-you-please', the audience is exclusively male, 'respectably' smoking and drinking. 'Several public houses possessed local champions – of a street, of a village – but these were emphatically not women ...' although 'it may be doubted whether a female clog-dancer had ever footed it in Bursley' the occasion is made respectable through the presence of Florence's husband. Nevertheless, Florence is immediately established as a sexu-al figure and a focus of male sexual tension by the attention to 'the shortness of her red and black velvet skirts, and the unde-niable complete visibility of her rounded calves'. Male status is confirmed in relation to her own, granting the chairman a superiority over his fiancee, the landlady of the public house, but causing Florence's own husband to assume a role of servi-tude and humiliation. She is described in regal terms, height-ening her position of superiority and unobtainability. Bennett places her in a position of tantalising sexual authori-ty which has a profound hold over the audience.

The gestures of Mr Offlow, and her gestures, as he arranged and prepared the surface of the little square danc-ing-board that was her throne, showed that he was the hus-band of Florence Simcox rather than she the wife of Offlow the reciter and dog-fancier. Further, it was his rôle to play the concertina to her: he had had to learn the concertina, possibly a secret humiliation for one whose judgement in terriers was not excelled in many public-houses.

> She danced; and the service-doorway showed a vista of open-mouthed scullions. There was no sound in the room, save the concertina and the champion clogs. Every eye was fixed on those clogs; even the little eyes of Mr Peake quitted the

button of his waistcoat and burned like diamond
points on those clogs. Florence herself chiefly
gazed on those clogs, but occasionally her noncha-
lant petulant gaze would wander up and down her
bare arms and across her bosom. At intervals, with
her ringed fingers she would lift the short skirt – a
nothing, an imperceptibility, half an inch, with
glance downcast; and the effect was profound,
recondite, inexplicable. Her style was not that of a
male clog-dancer, but it was indubitably clog-
dancing, full of marvels to the connoisseur, and to
the profane naught but a highly complicated
series of wooden noises.

As the dance progresses Bennett's language is increasingly sexual and the increasing excitement of the clog dance
becomes a metaphor for orgasm. The experience of the clog
dance symbolises Edwin Clayhanger's sexual awakening, his
transition from sixteen year-old schoolboy to manhood.

And then suddenly, the dancer threw up one foot
as high as her head and brought her two clogs
down together like a double mallet on the board,
and stood still. It was over.
    Mrs. Louisa Loggerheads turned nervously
away, pushing her servants in front of her. And
when the society of mutual buriers had recovered
from the startling shameless insolence of that last
high kick, it gave rein to its panting excitement,
and roared and stamped. Edwin was staggered.
The blood swept into his face, a hot tide. He was
ravished, but he was also staggered. He did not
know what to think of Florence, the champion
female clog-dancer. He felt that she was won-
drous; he felt that he could have gazed at her all
night; but he felt that she had put him under the
necessity of reconsidering some of his fundamen-
tal opinions.

But by placing Florence in the dominant sexual role,
Bennett must constantly reiterate her transgression of appropriate gender roles and he does this by portraying the female
clog dancer as an anomaly, emphasising the clog's associa-

tions with squalor, using it as a metaphor for prostitution. As a female clog act Florence is a 'daring item' – the only one to have appeared in the respectable confines of Bursley. She overshadows the only women in the room, who shun her, made nervous by her act which they turn instinctively away from. She has the confidence to stare down any man in the room and is accustomed to being regarded by audiences, an object of men's eyes. She is a pretty doll-like woman; with a show of bare flesh, jewels and golden ringlets she has none of the modesty or docility 'that Bursley was accustomed to think proper to the face of woman'. Her transformation of 'that which the instinct of the artist had taken from the sordid ugliness of the people' is achieved through her physical beauty, 'The clog, the very emblem of servitude and the squalor of brutalised populations, was changed, on the light feet of this favourite, into a medium of grace .... the clog meant everything that was harsh, foul and desolating; it summoned images of misery and disgust. Yet on those feet that had never worn it seriously, it became the magic instrument of pleasure .... putting upon everybody an enchantment.' Florence disguises squalor through beauty, she is the clog-dancing personification of the vamp or temptress leading men into a world of escape. Clog dancing becomes dangerous, subversive, threatening, offering a momentary illusion of escape from the reality of misery. Through his creation of Florence Simcox, Bennett unites the ugliness of the working-class with the transgression of woman emphasising two of the dominant fears of the Victorian capitalist patriarchy.

Bennett must have based his description of Florence Simcox on a real, closely-observed demonstration of clog-dancing. Many details correlate with accustomed clog dance conventions – the use of the portable, square, wooden dancing board. The silencing of the concertina during the complicated final figures of the dance and the mallet-like sound of the bringing down and the closing of the two feet together for the final step. The wearing of the short skirt rather than the traditional knee breeches must have been intended to emphasise Florence's femininity and sexual appeal.[42]

The women who took part in the Ladies' Contest must also have, whether consciously or unconsciously, exploited their sexual advantages in the eyes of a predominantly male jury. For instance, Nellie Coleman's persistent use of diminutives and false modesty increases her aura of feminine vulnerability and weakness, contradicting her clearly competitive ambitiousness as a clog dancer: 'I, Little Nellie Coleman'... 'Nellie Coleman, the Little Model' ... 'As the world is wide and I don't know everybody in it ... I have not won for myself title of Champion but hope to do so ...'

Contrary to the impression given by Arnold Bennett and Pat Tracey, there *were* many female clog dancers, but like Florence, they were subjected to a set of judgements based on gender roles and were not given the same status as equivalent male performers. Although they appear to have performed to the same criteria as male dancers with few differences in dancing style or competition rules, they were awarded lower prizes and achieved less renown. Female dancers were assessed mainly through physical appearance rather than on their merits as competitive dancers. Although the competition attracted bets, the odds were described in euphemistic terms – gambling was not a territory open to women. Many skilful female performers and champions remained on the periphery of success and earning potential due to the stereotyped confines of their gender and the incompatible symbolism of the clog.

It was due to its working-class associations that clog dancing lost its popularity. Although the main protagonists of the Ladies' Contest of 1898 went on to exploit the success won through the London match by obtaining bookings for a number of years afterwards, clog dancing could not retain its competitive status.

Soon after the turn of the twentieth century, clog dancing began a transformation from its tough, competitive form to a nostalgic and sentimental form, via two routes. An examination of a random selection of programmes from Glasgow music halls from 1900 and 1902 indicates the first route clog dancing was to take. Many of the women from the 1898 competition were busy fulfilling bookings, probably arranged soon after the match took place. At the Tivoli on 14 May 1900 we find Ada Dell – Comedienne, Coon and Clog Dancer. At the Britannia on 12 August, Minnie Ray – Champion Lady Clog Dancer of the World; 3 February 1902, Sisters Sullivan – Vocalists and Champion Lady Clog Dancers and on 3 March, Nellie Martell – Serio Comedienne and Dancer. But on 1 December 1902, a certain Maggie Walsh appeared at the

Lancashire Clogs by Emile Grimshaw, 1911, shows the
sentimentalised image of the clog dancing factory worker.

Sheet music: David Ebbage

Empire as 'The Singing Mill Girl'. Her act was one of a type that was to pave the way for the sentimental course that clog dancing was soon to take, heralding the mythologising of the 'industrial north'. The mill girl descended from the socially concerned factory dramas of the first half of the nineteenth century. But as the twentieth century dawned, the horrors of the Industrial Revolution receded, giving way to a new sentimental nineteenth-century image of Britain's changing industrial face. By the First World War, the clog – formerly favoured by the labouring classes – was becoming a thing of the past.

> Towards the later part of the war, higher wages and greater prosperity turned many people away from the use of clogs ... Men returning from the Army did not all take to clogs again. Moreover many of the pits were closing down, and conditions in some of the mills were changing ... Some people also appear to have regarded the wearing of clogs as being less distinguished socially than the use of boots and shoes.[43]

The image of the clog-wearing mill girl took a sentimental, nostalgic turn, with music, songs and musicals referring to a rose-tinted industrial heritage. The cover of the sheet music for 'Lancashire Clogs' a 'two step' for piano or orchestra published in 1911, illustrates a pair of Lancashire clogs and a cheerful, dancing couple of factory workers:[44] A later piece, 'The Clatter of the Clogs: A novelty fox-trot', from 1930 extends the myth of the happy factory worker.[45]

> C'lick, c'lack, c'lick, c'lack,
> There's music in the clatter of the clogs.
> There's rhythm in the sound of wooden shoes upon the
> ground,
> I love to hear the clatter of the clogs.
> And it echoes around ev'ry valley and hill
> In Lancashire "When they're off to the mill".
> The pit-a-pat of feet upon the cobbles on the street.
> There's music in the clatter of the clogs.
>
> See that throng, thousands strong
> toddle to work each morning

Lasses wearing shawls,
And hefty chaps in caps and overalls.
Near the mill hooters shrill,
Whistle a noisy warning, "Please be quick, you're late,
so hurry up before they shut the gate".

All day long the big mills hum.
Noisy bobbins whirl and strum
Spinning miles of cotton.
When there's a cotton boom
Busy fingers tend each loom,
And "Yarns" are spun in every room
Cares are all forgotten.

Tick-tock-tick time goes quick
Somebody gives the warning.
On go caps and shawls
And once again the noisy hooter calls.
"Work is done, off you run
'Till tomorrow morning"
Thro' the gates they pour
And the clogs begin to sing once more ...

However, by the end of the Second World War the sentimental myth of the mill girl had been replaced by the reality
of the munitions worker and the land girl. As Britain sought
to regenerate itself there was little reason to look back at the
Industrial Revolution with its grim associations. Clog dancing was all but forgotten by the older generation; many
dancers were ashamed to refer to their past art, condemning
their steps to their memories, refusing to share them with
researchers from the clog dancing revival of the 1970s.

The lasting impression of clog dancing remains that of the
Dutch dancer. This was created by the many juvenile dancers
who attended the popular dancing schools set up by amateurs
and professionals throughout the country. Most dancing
schools taught the 'Lancashire Hornpipe' in clogs. This was
based on the so-called 'seven steps' integral to Lancashire
clog. This, in turn, was replaced by the easier 'sailors' hornpipe' which could be danced with or without clogs. The
'sailors' hornpipe' was one of an increasing number of character dances that began to be favoured over the straight, com-

Miss Sophie Jones, The Champion Baby Clog Dancer,
dressed in the baggy breeches of the Dutch character
dance whilst displaying the clogs and trophies of the
Lancashire competition dance. Postcard, n.d.

Author's collection

petition clog dance.

It is possible that in the light of the evidence considered throughout this paper, the character dance was considered more suitable for a child with terpsichorean ambitions than the contentious and quarrelsome competition clog dance. But the character dance that achieved most popularity was the 'Dutch Dance', performed in a charming Dutch costume with large wooden clogs obtained from a theatrical outfitters. It was performed to tunes such as 'By the Side of the Zuyder Zee', or 'Little Mister Baggy Breeches'.[46] As the juvenile pupils matured, they transferred their skills back into the music halls, and the Dutch Dance took its place alongside other variety acts suitable to a new audience, composed less exclusively of the working class and more of a new, 'respectable', 'lower-middle-class'. Miss Sophie Jones, 'The Champion Baby Clog Dancer' demonstrates the transition from the old-style competition dancer to the character dancer dressed in the baggy breeches of the Dutch Dance; but she is still sporting the decorative, Lancashire 'dandy clogs' favoured by the competition dancer. Eva Johnson and her music hall partner chose to be illustrated on their publicity card as a Dutch couple; but although their clogs are cleverly disguised as large, wooden ones, they too are the old Lancashire style originally worn by the cotton weavers. It was only when dancers finally shed the industrial wood and leather clog and donned the metal plated tap shoes of the jazz age that clog dancing finally bid its farewell to the music halls of Britain.

Notes

1.   Part of this essay was first published in the proceedings of the fifth Study of Dance Conference at the University of Surrey, Guildford, England 20–23 April 1995. See Caroline Kershaw, '"They've Done Me, They've Robbed Me, but, Thank God, I'm the Champion Still": Clog Dancing in the Victorian Music Hall,' in Prof. Janet Adshead-Lansdale, ed., *Border Tensions: Dance and Discourse* (Guildford: Dept of Dance Studies, University of Surrey, 1995).
2.   R.U. Sayce, 'Pattens and Clogs,' *Transactions of the Rochdale Literary and Scientific Society*. XXI (1941–43), pp. 46–51. Manchester Local Studies Collection, Manchester Public Library.
3.   See J.S Bratton: 'Dancing a Hornpipe in Fetters,' *Folk Music Journal*, 6:1 (1990), 65–82.
4.   Dates not given. A present day dancer from an unbroken family line of Lancashire clog dancers, Pat Tracey traces her steps back via her grandfather to the 1820s, but believes them to have originated in the late eighteenth century.
5.   See Patricia Tracey, 'The Lancashire Hornpipe,' in Prof. Janet Adshead-

Lansdale, ed., *The Hornpipe: Proceedings of the National Early Music Association Conference 1993* (Cambridge: National Early Music Association, 1993) pp. 15–22.

6. Dates not given. According to Pat Tracey, Bill Gibbons was born in the late 1890s in Burscough, living and working on the Leeds-Liverpool canal where he learnt his steps as a bargeman.

7. See *Era*, 16 October 1897, p. 20 for details of the 1880 contest. My forthcoming doctoral thesis on Dan Leno discusses the clog contests. Also see my article, Caroline Kershaw, 'Dan Leno: New Evidence on Early Influences and Style in Nineteenth Century Theatre,' *Nineteenth Century Theatre*, 22:1 (Summer 1994), 30–55.

8. The finals took place on Saturday 12 February 1898 at the People's Empire music hall, Bow, London. The winner was George Burns from Glasgow, whose clog dancing career was later cut short when he was run over by a tram in Trongate, losing a leg in 1899. A biograph film was made of the finals but does not appear to have survived.

9. *Era*, 22 January, 1898, p. 31.

10. *Ibid.*, 5 February, 1898, p. 31.

11. *Ibid.*, 29 January, 1898, p. 20.

12. *Ibid.*, p.34.

13. *Ibid.*, 5 February, 1898, p. 31.

14. *Ibid.*

15. Many clog dancers hollowed out holes in the heels of the clogs in which coins or brass 'jingles' were deposited, sealing them in with a brass plate. These created an impression of more beats being added to the steps and were never allowed in competitions where the number of beats was always carefully monitored. Other dancers simply attached a metal plate to their heels, similar to modern taps to accentuate the beats.

16. *Era*, 12 February, 1898, p.26.

17. See Tracey, 'The Lancashire Hornpipe,' p. 16.

18. An American tutor published at the height of the clog dancing craze in 1873 shows that there were an equivalent number of female clog dancers in America. See Anthony G. Barrand, Kathryn Kari Smith and Rhett Krause, ed., *Jig and Clog Dancing Without a Master: The Clifford (1864), Buckley (1869) and James (1873) Manuals: Volume II: Source Texts and Illustrations* (Brattleboro, VT: Northern Harmony Publishing Company, 1994). The song-and-dance and jig and clog dancers among the ladies in the profession are: Lotta, Jenny Worrell, Jenny Yeamans, Little Rosebud, Kitty O'Neil, Jenny Benson, Baby Benson, Nellie Howard, Annie Gibbons, Patti Rosa, Sadie Seagrist. Hattie Grinnell, French Twin Sisters, Ida Siddons, Polly McDonald, Mlle. Eugenia, Fanny Lacelle, Mlle. Baretta, Fanny Beane, Jenny Miaeo, Emma La Mause, Sallie St. Clair etc., pp. 6–7.

19. Description of Dan Leno in a review for *Era*, 29 September, 1888, p. 15.

20. *Ibid.*, 9 April 1898, p.27; 30 April 1898, p. 19.

21. *Variety*, 1:13, 7 May 1898, p. 8.

22. *Era*, 16 October, 1897, p. 20.

23. The match between Ray and Perman took place at the London Pavilion on Wednesday 29 June 1898. See *Era*, 2 July, 1898, p.17 for details of the competition and dancers.

24. *Ibid.*, p. 5.

25. *Ibid.* & *Variety*, 1:12, 30 April, 1898, p. 12.

26. Charles Chaplin, *My Autobiography* (Harmondsworth, Middx: Penguin, 1987),

pp. 43–50.

27. *Magnet,* 14 July 1900, quoted in David Robinson, *Chaplin His Life and Art* (London: Paladin, 1986), p. 29.

28. Glasgow Empire, 18 February 1901. Music Hall programmes 1900/1901 and Account Book held in Mitchell Collection, Glasgow. Chaplin was no longer in the troupe.

29. See Anon., 'Actual Stepdancing': Sam Sherry; an autobiography,' *Call Boy* (Spring 1980), p.12; Eddie Flaherty, 'Memories of a Lancashire Clog Dancer,' *English Dance and Song*, XXX: 2 (Summer 1968), 42–43 and Hickory Wood, *Dan Leno* (London: Methuen, 1904), pp.72–73 for descriptions of the training of juvenile clog dancers.

30. Sophie Jones displays both a cup and a medal.

31. For pictorial examples of the standard Lancashire costume see Anthony G. Barrand, PhD. and Kathryn Kari A. Smith, *The Dancing Marleys: A New England Family Tradition of 'Lancashire Clog': Issues of Ethnicity and Family Identity in American Wooden Shoe Dancing.* (Brattleboro, VT: Private publication Dr. Anthony G. Barrand, 1993), p. 14.

32. *Variety*, 1:13, 23 April, 1898, p. 12.

33. *Era*, 21 May, 1898, p. 20.

34. Tracy C. Davis, *Actresses as Working Women: Their social identity in Victorian culture* (London: Routledge, 1991), p.105.

35. Bratton, 'Dancing a Hornpipe in Fetters,' pp. 70–71.

36. *Variety*, 1:11, 23 April, 1898, p. 12.

37. See my 'They've done me, they've robbed me ...' for a fuller discussion of class associations and clog dancing.

38. Tracey, 'The Lancashire Hornpipe,' p. 16.

39. Transcript from *Woman's Hour*, BBC Radio 4, 1 May, 2000.

40. See the Instep team's Newcastle Series of booklets of clog steps, often containing biographical information on individual dancers. Metherell Collection.

41. Arnold Bennett, *Clayhanger* (London: Methuen, 1962).

42. Aylis Angus (a step dancer born c.1923, from a travelling family in the Northumberland and Newcastle area), states that she wore a crimson skirt, a navy satin blouse and crimson clogs for public display and competitions; 'You're going to attract the judge's eye and get more points if you wave your skirts about and show a bit of leg'. See Ednie Wilson, *Aylis Angus: Step Dancer*, Newcastle Series. (Newcastle: Instep, ND).

43. Sayce, 'Pattens and Clogs,' p. 50.

44. Emile Grimshaw, *Lancashire Clogs: Two Step* (London: Hawkes and Son, 1911). David Ebbage Collection.

45. Howard Flynn, arr. Tom Blight, *The Clatter of the Clogs: A Novelty Fox-Trot* (London: Billy Thorburn Publishing Co. Ltd, 1930. David Ebbage Collection.

46. See Julian Pilling, *The Lancashire Clog Dance* (London: English Folk Dance and Song Society, 1967), pp. 5–6.

Further reading

Anon, 'Actual Stepdancing: Sam Sherry, an autobiography,' *Call Boy*, Spring 1980.

Barrand, Anthony G., PhD. and Smith, Kathryn Kari A. *The Dancing Marleys. A New England Family Tradition of*

'*Lancashire' Clog: Issues of Ethnicity and Family Identity in American Wooden Shoe Dancing*. Brattleboro, VT: Private Publication, 1993.

Bennett, Arnold, *Clayhanger,* originally published 1910.

Bratton, J.S. 'Dancing a Hornpipe in Fetters,' *Folk Music Journal* 6:1. (1990), pp. 65–82.

Chaplin, Charles, *My Autobiography,* Harmondsworth, Middx: Penguin, 1987.

Flaherty, Eddie, 'Memories of a Lancashire Clog Dancer,' *English Dance and Song*, XXX:2 (Summer 1968), 42-43.

Flett, J.F. & T.M., *Traditional Step-Dancing in Lakeland*. London: English Folk Dance and Song Society, 1979.

Kershaw, Caroline, 'Dan Leno: New Evidence of Early Influences and Style,' *Nineteenth Century Theatre* 22:1 (1994), pp. 30–55.

Kershaw, Caroline, '"They've Done Me, They've Robbed Me, but, Thank God, I'm the Champion Still": Clog Dancing in the Victorian Music Hall,' in Prof. Janet Adshead-Lansdale, ed., *Border Tensions: Dance and Discourse*, Guildford: Dept. of Dance Studies, University of Surrey, 1995.

Inglehearn, Madeleine, 'The hornpipe, our national dance?' in NEMA *The Hornpipe*, pp. 37–50. National Early Music Association (NEMA) *The Hornpipe* conference papers, 1993.

Jig and Clog Dancing Without a Master: The Clifford (1864), Buckley (1869) and James (1873) Manuals. Volume II: Source Texts and Illustrations. Eds. Anthony G. Barrand, Kathryn Karl Smith and Rhett Krause. Northern Harmony Publishing Company. Brattleboro, VT. U.S.A. 1994.

Metherell, Chris, *An Introductory Bibliography on Clog and Step Dance*. Vaughan Williams Memorial Library Leaflet no.22. London: English Folk Dance and Song Society, 1994.

Newcastle Series. Various booklets on clog steps. Instep Publications. n.d.

Pilling, Julian, *The Lancashire Clog Dance*. London: English Folk Dance and Song Society, 1967.

Robinson, David, *Chaplin His Life and Art,* London: Paladin, 1986.

Sayce, R.U., 'Pattens and Clogs,' *Transactions of the Rochdale Literary and Scientific Society*, XXI (1941–43), 1942; 46–51.

Tracey, Patricia, 'The Lancashire Hornpipe,' in Prof. Janet
    Adshead-Lansdale, ed., *The Hornpipe: Proceedings of the
    National Early Music Association Conference 1993*.
    Cambridge: National Early Music Association, 1993, pp.
    15–22.
Wood, Hickory. J, *Dan Leno,* London: Methuen, 1905.

Silhouette of William Castle. No original has been traced
of this reproduction from Alfred Beesley's additionally
illustrated copy of the *History of Banbury* (1841), in the
Centre for Oxfordshire Studies, Oxford Library, (Vol. 12,
p.101). It bears the caption 'William Castle, called Mettle,
a half idiot, started by the Populace as Opposition
candidate in 1820'.

'A Very Celebrated Banbury Character': Reconstructing working class biography – the case of William 'Old Mettle' Castle

Keith Chandler

One truism of research is that individual members of the working class rarely leave much of a mark on the pages of history; and the farther back in time, the less possible it becomes to flesh out such lives. A small number left behind diaries or, more rarely, autobiographies, some of which have survived into the modern era. For the past four hundred years for most, though by no means all, we have registrations of baptism, marriage, baptisms of children, and burial. And, since 1841, the vast majority have been chronicled in the decadal censuses. Such entries in civil and ecclesiastical records freeze a few moments in time and space for posterity, but the minutiae of day-to-day existence remain largely undocumented.

Once in a while, however, a working man leads such an unusual and colourful life that he features in a great number of contemporary and posthumous sources. One such life – that of William 'Old Mettle' Castle – is placed under scrutiny in this piece. The situation offers a rare opportunity for the historian to allow the primary sources (given here verbatim, retaining original spelling, indention, punctuation, etc) to convey their own story, with merely a minimum degree of commentary and interpretation.

As it happens, our subject leaves fewer impressions than most in those official sources which are the lifeblood of the historian. He died mere days before the taking of the first detailed nationwide census; leaves no trace of personal schooling or religious conviction (if such existed); apparently never married or produced children; as a non-householder had no right to vote, even after electoral reform; nor left a will. Yet from the less conventional (and more vibrant) evidence which survives, many revealing insights into the social, criminal, political and cultural life of a north Oxfordshire market town during the first half of the nineteenth century, as reflected in the experiences of one inhabitant, are laid bare.

There is certainly a suggestion that he may have worked the canal barges before the accident which crippled him;[1] although elsewhere the accident is said to have occurred in 'early childhood',[2] which would make such employment unlikely, or at the very least limited. One source speaks of him being at 'a considerable distance' from Banbury,[3] and another, ambiguously, in a 'distant part of the county on a boating expedition or something of the kind',[4] both referring to the year 1818 or later. But, while allowing for the obvious paucity and bias of sources, from the locations named we may observe that Castle's life was played out almost entirely within a few miles of Banbury itself.

He resided variously in the village of his birth, Adderbury (three miles to the south), from 1793 to probably 1799 and beyond, presumably in a cottage; on an 'old boat' moored at Neithrop (to the north and west of the town centre), around 1830, and Grimsbury (a mile just east of north), in 1841. He was also said to have slept at times in lodging houses, barns and 'hovels'.[5]

He was active in the role of fool to morris dance sets based at Adderbury, Bloxham (also three miles to the south) and Kings Sutton (four miles south-east). In that capacity he would have travelled with the dancers to various villages – almost certainly including Souldern (seven miles south-east) – for the club feasts and other festivities, but all this would have occurred probably within, say, ten miles of Banbury. Castle's known criminal activities extended as far as Shutford (four miles west), and as a result he made his longest recorded journeys, on two occasions (in 1830 and 1831), to Oxford gaol and assizes, a distance of some twenty-three or -four miles. Other than Grimsbury and Shutford (this latter on the same parallel), all of these locations lie to the south of Banbury, and no firm evidence survives to indicate that Castle ever travelled further northwards.

At this remove we have to make an effort to imagine the physical context of life prior to 1841, especially in what was essentially an insular and parochial community, albeit one on the threshold of drastic social transition. C.R. Cheney, in the Introduction to *Shoemaker's Window*,[6] written in 1948, gives some flavour of the period:

> Herbert shows us Banbury before the Reform Bill, Banbury before the railway came to it, Banbury unpaved and unlighted, its streets encumbered with piles of timber and other odorous obstacles and bisected in some places by channels of filthy water across which foot-passengers made their way on stepping-stones. But because of these features we must not suppose that life was stagnant in the little town. The borough with its adjacent hamlets contained between five and six thousand inhabitants when George Herbert was born [*1814*], and the population was steadily growing. Even if the North family interest usually determined the votes of the eighteen or so electors to Banbury's parliamentary seat, elections were occasionally contested and excited popular interest, even disorder. Although no railway touched Banbury until 1850, there was an impressive timetable of regular coaches and wagons which maintained contact with the larger towns of the West Midlands and with London. Already in 1825 a scheme was set on foot for paving and lighting the streets and Herbert has a good deal to tell of the execution of this work.

Some of the sources about Castle that I reproduce come from contemporary personal observation, even first-hand interaction with Castle himself, and some from the oral tradition. Each piece reflects the prejudices and perceptions of the commentator. Some are sympathetic towards Castle's unconventional lifestyle, others are condemnatory. A very few, including George Herbert, saw through the lunatic image Castle fostered around himself, to the native intelligence and guile beneath.

Primary sources that clarify and put into context Castle's life but do not mention him by name (excepting those that unambiguously refer to him anyway) are italicised. My commentary on sources is presented in italics in square brackets.

A Life:

Wednesday, 30 January 1793
The real name of this eccentric person was William Castle: he was of an Adderbury family, and born about the year 1789.[7]

[William Castle was baptised at Adderbury on Wednesday, 30 January 1793, the son of John and Ann Castle. It was frequently the case that baptism occurred two or three weeks after birth, although longer and shorter periods are recorded. William Castle was therefore probably born in early January. At the date of their marriage on Saturday, 3 November 1792 John was aged 22, a weaver living in Adderbury West, and Ann (née Gunn), aged 29 and living in Adderbury East (the village straddles the main Oxford Road). It is a well documented fact that, during this period, individuals often did not know their exact age and date of birth. The disparity of the year of birth given in the 1841 source quoted above – 1789 – and the more likely 1793, clearly stems from the general belief that Castle was '52 or 53' at the time of death.[8]]

Tuesday, 10 September 1799
[The burial of John Castle, presumably William's father (although generally before 1813 ages at the time of death were seldom entered in burial registers, so identification cannot be confirmed beyond any doubt) is recorded at Adderbury on Tuesday, 10 September 1799. Although he later occasionally mentioned a brother in response to questions about why he acted the fool, there is no evidence for any siblings in the official sources. If, as seems likely, the widow and child were left alone and unprovided for, this goes some way towards explaining Castle's subsequent rambling and independent

existence. Both parents would, however, have possessed an extend-
ed local family network, and it was usually the case that relatives
would take in those who found themselves in such hardship.]

Probably 1800–1820

In his early childhood he experienced an accident which
occasioned such deformity of his legs as to render him incapable of hard and steady labour.[9]

An accident, which happened to him in early life, had injured
his legs so much as to render him incapable of hard labour –
to which he never professed any very strong attachment.[10]

Another source says that Old Mettle was a canal boatman and
that he became lame because his leg was caught between two
barges. He then earned a living by selling sulphur matches.[11]

1818

Mettle's chief fame arose, however from his being put forward, by the people of Banbury, as the candidate in opposition to the Guildford interest, at all the elections which
occurred between 1818 and 1831; but, in the latter year, Mr.
Easthope, and, subsequently, Mr. Tancred, were set up in
Mettle's place ... In 1818, Mettle was the opponent of the late
lamented and beloved Hon. Frederick Sylvester North
Douglas.[12]

BANBURY. THE BOROUGH. – There lives a person who,
many years ago, was a frequent mock-candidate for the honour of representing Banbury in Parliament. This person is
Mr. Mettle. We well remember the time when poor Mettle
used to climb upon the Town Hall steps, and harangue the
gaping multitude after this fashion: – "Gentlemen, you shall
none of you do no work when I go to Parliament, and you
shall all have a half-peck loaf for fourpence." The eloquence
of Mettle was usually received with unbounded applause; but
unfortunately his benevolent views lacked discernment in
one particular – for Mettle could never point out the way in
which those persons who *were to do no work* could come by the
fourpences to buy their loaves with. Just such a scheme is that
of the Whigs and Mr. Tancred, for ruining the town and trade
of Banbury, and then mocking the people with the offer of

cheap bad bread, which they could find no fourpences to pay for! As the scheme of Mettle, and that of the Whigs and Mr. Tancred, are thus identical, we submit to the public that, in common justice, Mettle, as being the original inventor, ought to have the credit of it: and though he was formerly but a mock-candidate, his prior claims being considered, we think he ought now be brought forward as a real candidate for Banbury. The fictitious estate in Yatesbury might surely do for Mettle as well as it has done for Mr. Tancred. Besides, there is something in Dean Swift's witty advice concerning his countrymen. "If," he says, "we are to have blockheads, at least give us leave to have *our own* blockheads." A blockhead, Mettle may be, and very likely is; but, upon the witty Dean's own shewing, if Mettle were to contend with Tancred, he oufi-ht [*ought*] to win in a canter.[13]

[*This is a typical piece of contemporary political satire. There would certainly never have been any serious intention of putting Castle up as a candidate for Parliament. For a similarly pitched response see the entry for May 1841, below. Castle's candidacy between 1818 and 1830 would have had many psychological and social aspects. Among the former was legitimate political expression by the disenfranchised which was sanctioned, even encouraged (see quote immediately following), by the establishment. And among the latter were sheer frolics, parades, dressing up, wearing favours of ribbons or 'deal shavings' – and plenty of free beer. Although none is mentioned in any of the primary sources for Banbury, political rallies and elections during this period often featured one or more bands playing music through the streets.*]

At a former period he was a remarkably popular person at the Borough Elections; and he has sometimes been sent for from a considerable distance on these occasions. No candidate was, at these times, suffered to be chaired, except in company with Mr. Mettle, with which honour the said candidates, of course, expressed themselves to be most exceedingly delighted and gratified![14]

November 1819
On the death of that gentleman [*Frederick Sylvester North Douglas*] in 1819, Mettle was a second time a candidate for Banbury, in opposition to the Hon. Heneage Legge. Mettle's

colours were deal shavings, which the ladies of the Banbury
Rads most industriously made up into favours.[15]

*In November, 1819 the Hon. Heneage Legge was elected in the
Tory interest and was chaired through the streets with the usual
distribution of favours and beer.*[16]

Friday, 10 March 1820
The death of George the Third caused another election within two or three months; on which occasion Mettle's supporters had increased so vastly in numbers and violence, that a
riot ensued ... On this or an after occasion, Mettle, who was in
a distant part of the county on a boating expedition or something of the kind, was considered to be out of all possible
reach of getting to the hustings on time; but he was sent for
express, brought by coach more than a hundred miles, and,
just before the poll, was borne into the town in triumph on
the shoulders of his friends.[17]

On Friday the 10th inst. being the day appointed for the election of a Member of Parliament for this borough, a large con-
course of people assembled, and it being generally
understood that the usual practice of distributing beer and
ribbons to the populace was to be discontinued, the persons
assembled soon began to shew strong symptoms of disappro-
bation, by hissing, groaning, &c. and many of them paraded
the streets with favours, made of deal shavings, in their hats.
Whilst this was going on, a party proceeded to the White Lion
Inn, and took possession of an old chaise, in which they
placed a poor half-witted fellow, nick-named Mettel, and
drew him to the Mayor's house, crying "Mettle for ever!" –
"No Legge!" A few stones were thrown through the Mayor's
windows. The chaise was then placed in front of the Town
Hall.[18]

*The Hon. Heneage Legge was elected Member of Parliament in this
year. There was a great row at the election. When the Corporation
went into the Town Hall to complete the election the crowd collected round the building and became exceedingly riotous, sending a
shower of stones at the Town Hall windows. It had been intimated
that there would not be so much beer given away as formerly, which
enraged the mob. The Corporation tried to mend matters by offer-*

*ing beer, but this peace offering they then refused to accept.
Bloxham, the sheriff's officer, put his head out of window holding a
jug in his hand, and called out "Plenty of beer! plenty of beer!" but a
shower of stones made him speedily withdraw. Two men then
appeared carrying a large tub of beer slung on a pole; this the mob
poured down a drain in the Market Place. The pebbles with which
the Market Place was paved were turned up and used as missiles,
the windows of the Town Hall being completely smashed. The mob
threatened to pull the Town Hall down, with the Corporation
inside it, and began picking at the pillars which supported it. The
Rev. T.W. Lancaster, the Vicar of Banbury, who was a member of
the corporate body, climbed into a sort of cock-loft under the clock,
this did not bear his weight, and he went through, but happening to
bestride a joist, he sat there with his legs dangling through the ceiling. One by one the members managed to steal away. Mr. William
Walford got out and was walking across Corn Hill when half a
brick, part of the Town Hall, hit him in the back, and he managed
to get into the Plough Inn. Many others were hurt, and much riot-
ing continued all day and night.*[19]

In March following Parliament was dissolved and Mr. Legge
had to seek re-election. He announced on this occasion he
could not afford the expenses attached to the usual demonstrations and the election must proceed without them.

This Disappointed and angered the populace and they
proceeded to demonstrate accordingly.

They obtained a post chaise and put old Mettle in it. This
was a well-known character, who sold home-made matches in
the town, clad in a collegian's cap and gown. They paraded
him as their elected member, stopping at the Town Hall in the
Market Place where the Council was proceeding with the
election of Legge.

They surrounded the Town Hall and became exceedingly
riotous. The Council tried to mend matters by offering them
beer and two men appeared carrying a large tub full of it
which the mob poured down a drain. The pebbles with which
the Market Place was paved were torn up and every window
of the Hall was broken. They began to pick at the pillars supporting the Hall in execution of their threat to destroy it.

The Councillors were in a great state of alarm and tried to
escape. The Rev. T.W. Lancaster, the Vicar of Banbury,
climbed into a little chamber beneath the clock, but the lath

and plaster would not bear his weight and he fell through and would have crashed into the hall but he happened to bestride a beam with his legs dangling through the ceiling. Mr. W. Walford, the Town Clerk, was struck by a brick in the Cornhill and just managed to reach the Plough Inn.

Meanwhile the crowd had been drawn off by their mistaking Mr. Timothy Cobb, the banker, for the member, to whom he bore some resemblance. They chased him up Butcher's Row to the bank in High Street which he managed to reach, while Mr. Legge got to the Red Lion and escaped in a chaise ...[20]

Circa 1823 or 1824

... as we lived in the London Yard and our house at the back was in the churchyard, I was a great deal with Briner and old Mettle. When Briner got old he employed old Mettle to dig the graves, so you will see now how it was that I knew so much of these two curious characters.[21]

[*George Herbert was born in 1814, and aged 9½ when living in London Yard*].

I come now in order of the church officials to the Dog-whipper whose name was Briner. [An official formerly employed to whip dogs out of a church or chapel, locally retained, to mean a sexton or beadle – O.E.D.] His office was to attend in front of the church to see to the chiming of the bells for church and the winding up of the clock and chimes and the digging of the graves, attending to the churchyard, lighting the fires under the church for heating purposes, etc.[22]

Saturday, 10 June 1826

In 1826, on two different occasions, Mettle was the opponent of the Hon. A.C. Legge.[23]

GENERAL ELECTION – On Saturday last the Hon. Arthur C. Legge was unanimously re-elected for the borough of Banbury. The Hon. Member was chaired amidst the acclamations of the surrounding multitude, and the day passed off with the greatest good humour and hilarity.[24]

June–September 1827
When the small pox raged at Banbury in 1827, Mettle was the
constant and fearless nightly burier of the dead.[25]

*I will endeavour to describe the fair which took place when that
dreadful calamity fell upon the town, and the small-pox came upon
us. It was at a Twelfth Fair. This was as large a fair at this time as
was the Michaelmas Fair, but was a pleasure fair entirely, and
there were a lot of shows and other amusements. In one of these
shows was a camera obscura: this was quite a new sight at fairs and
obtained a large amount of patronage, but in another part of this
same show was a man dead with the small-pox, unknown to the
people who visited it, and this was how so many caught the disease,
not only in the town but in the neighbourhood.[26]*

*According to the Parish Register of 1827, 73 persons died of the
small-pox in that year. The infection was brought into the town at
the Holy Thursday Fair-not Twelfth Fair which was, and still is, a
horse fair. Michaelmas Fair was a hiring fair, or "mop", and has
been also a great pleasure fair up the present day.[27]*

[*The epidemic raged through the town between June and
September.*]

Probably 1820s or 1830s
One of the most remarkable characters living in Banbury
sixty years ago was a man named William Castle, who always
went by the name of "Old Metal." He was a born comedian,
full of oddities of speech and drollery. His name was a terror
to children to whom he was known as "the Bogieman."[28]

"Old Mettle" was a well-known character. He lived in a lodging house and frequently wore a college cap and gown. He
was a very odd-looking man, with his mouth always half
open, and one of his legs very much bent; and made his living
by splitting wood into matches and dipping the ends in brimstone. These he hawked about the street, carrying a bundle of
them on the end of a stick over his shoulder, and sold a penny
worth or halfpenny worth to his customers. He frequently
rested himself upon people's door-steps. One day when on
ours, with his matches by him, I recollect my father asking
him why he made such a fool of himself, when he looked up at

my father with his usual vacant smile, and said, – "Why, sir; I beant sich a fool as I looks. I've got a brother as works 'ard for his livin', and nobody never gies him half a pint, but they gie me lots every day."[29]

Mettle had a way of living by his wits, and, so that his crooked stumps would but carry him from village-wake to village-wake, where he might amuse the gaping crowds around him by playing the fool, nobody was so happy, nor anybody so independent, as he! So long and so well did Mettle ape the fool, that most persons considered him for years as really being a fool. His ostensible trade, when not engaged at merry-makings, was that which Mettle himself would dignify by the appellation of "carver and gilder," although many persons would confer upon it an humbler name. When he was believed to be a fool, it was a very common thing for persons to try to play tricks upon him ... Another person one day told Mettle that he was a fool. Mettle replied, there was always one fool in every family, but it was his brother, and not he, that was the fool of his family, for his brother went to work![30]

"Old Metal" again was another celebrity. You speak of him as a "born comedian". The late Mr Cadbury [*James Cadbury, a member of Banbury Corporation*], I have been told, once said to him "Friend, though art a greater k than f". Most folks would agree with that. The man was originally a canal boatman; his leg was once caught between the tow-rope of two passing barges, and so severely lacerated that he was lamed for life. He then started as a brimstone match vender, a collector of trifles of "old metal", and a buffoon generally. Mrs John Cheney Sr. has an excellent portrait of him painted by our much-esteemed old friend, her late husband.[31]

[*The final sentence here refers to a painting by John Cheney in 1840 (oil on canvas, approximately 7 x 11 inches) which now hangs in Banbury Museum. A handwritten sheet of paper slipped into the frame alcove at the rear of the canvas (the text of which immediately follows this note) states, however, that the artist was Joseph Scarcebrook. Prior to Castle's death, Cheney, a local printer, had an engraving made of the painted image, and printed copies for sale, and perhaps the engraving was the work of Scarcebrook. Another source (see below) ascribes the painting to one Mr Levy.*

A commercially produced lithograph, probably 1840,
based on an original oil painting in Banbury Museum.

Janet Blunt of Adderbury possessed a copy of the lithograph, which she sent to Cecil Sharp.[32] On Monday, 28 April 1986 I interviewed Frederick and Winifred G. Wyatt in their home at Adderbury. She had been maid to Janet Blunt, and after her death had rescued the manuscripts relating to dance and song collected by Blunt during the first quarter of the twentieth century – before relatives burned everything they considered worthless – and posted them directly to the English Folk Dance and Song Society in London. She showed me an original painting (on wood, about 9 x 12 inches), lacquered and fading with age into an overall brown, and very similar to the copy in Banbury Museum – on which the lithograph Blunt sent to Sharp was based. On the back of the painting, in Blunt's handwriting, was the legend: 'This picture was given to Miss Janet H Blunt of Adderbury Manor. Oxon by Mrs Joseph Welch senior of West Adderbury ... Old Metal was the fool of the Morris [illegible word] side in which William Walton. His [illegible word] was George Castle.']

This Sketch by Joseph Scarcebrook is a fair likeness of William Castle an eccentric man who lived for many years in Banbury and was well known to the writer and to most of the Inhabitants of the Town both old and young as "Old Metal." this was at the time when the Tinder-box, Flint & Steel were in use for striking a light, and this man got his living by making the kind of matches then used, and hawking them round the Town dressed in the garb as represented, but he did not knock at the doors as most other sellers of matches did, but tied a few on the end of a stick and held them up to the windows & made a funny noise as he went past, the people then either sent or went out to buy the matches they required.[33]

I will now tell you something about old Mettle. He was always supposed to be what the Scotch call "daft," that is, I suppose, what we call "silly," but I know better than that. He was no more daft than I am, but he knew how to make himself appear so. When you knew him well, he could converse with you as well as any one, but old Mettle knew how his bread was buttered and he would make himself appear as big a fool as he pleased.[34]

He was fond of obtaining any grotesque piece of apparel – sometimes a cocked hat; sometimes a trencher cap and college gown ... and sometimes a lady's curls, surmounted by a straw bonnet and flowers, adorned his face.[35]

Mettle's favourite dress was of the oddest patchwork sort that he could put together. Sometimes he wore a huge cocked hat like a beadle. On another occasion, a straw hat or bonnet of enormous dimensions, which some un-English lady had brought from Paris. On two occasions, and two only, he assumed a graver garb. In one instance, some wag of the University of Oxford gave him a cap and gown, in which Mettle did not fail to go about, and in which he stood for his portrait to Mr. Levy, which was lithographed, and it is now a rare and precious gem in the collections of the curious.[36]

One of Mettle's occasional avocations, at fairs and such like times, was to receive from the beggars and other meagre itinerants such of their children as they could not lug about in the crowd: these he took great care of, laid the quiet ones down on the floor, and took up each squalling one in turn and handled it like a parent. – sympathy with his own class was also deeply shewn by many a halfpenny of Mettle's (too often the last he possessed) being bestowed upon some wretched wayfarer ... Yet, possessing these kind qualities, Mettle was, from his singular appearance and habits, made the bugbear of the town and neighbourhood, and every young person of this vicinity, whose age does not exceed twenty-five years, must remember being tortured and *ruled* in infancy by the parental threat – "Mettle shall have you!"[37]

He was also an enormous chewer of tobacco. This he also used to beg. I once saw him coming up Parson's Street, and he met at the corner of Church Lane Mr. Mallam, and Mr. C. Page used at that time to keep a grocer's and seedsman's shop. Old Mettle met them gossiping at the shop-door, and Mettle says to Mr. Page "Give us a bit of baccie, Master." Mr. Page walked into his shop and took down his tobacco-jar and says, "Open your mouth, old fellow," and he put into his mouth as much as ever he could get in, and Mallam then up with his stick and crammed it in tighter. Such were the jokes that Mettle liked to have played upon him.[38]

You know how he used to dress in an old collegian's gown and

trencher-cap and go about the streets with a bunch of matches stuck upon the end of his stick, and carry this across his
shoulder. These matches he used to make himself. He would
beg his wood at any carpenter's shop, and his brimstone for
dipping the matches he could always beg of one of the iron-
mongers, so you see his was all profit.[39]

His ostensible mode of gaining a livelihood was by selling
matches, but we believe he relied more upon the clearings of
pantries of those who were inclined to befriend him, than
upon his own exertions.[40]

Ought not to forget Old Mettle who used to be up in the Morn
to go his rounds into peoples front gardens in search of his
daintes [*dainty?*] Snails when the boys teased him he would
swing round his rod with its line and tail at the end like a
Corn Therhers [*Thresher's*] Flail with such a Whack unto
their backs make them squeal Oh Mettle have you been stung
by a Nettle or has a Bee settled on your Knee.[41]

"Old Mettle" made + sold, – rush-lights, for his living – he
"peddled" all about the district, and lived rather anyhow, in
barns + hovels; + at last was found dead on the road to
Banbury from here [*Adderbury*]. This is a bundle of rush-
lights he is carrying on his stick – just as he did in his wan-
derings; but I gathered from old W. Walton that he used to
flick the onlookers with a bladder on a cow-tail when he went
with the Morris Men as the Fool; but wore this queer dress
then ... Taplin, of the Dealer's Shop where I got it, said, "He
O.M. was a very Celebrated Banbury character in old days –"[42]

[*William Walton (1837–1919) was the last leader of the Adderbury
Morris Dancers. His father, also William Walton (1806–1848),
had been leader before him, and it must be this earlier period to
which the younger Walton's anecdotes relate, as he himself would
have been only four years old when Castle died.*]

Circa 1830s
Besides this he was foremost at all the merry-makings and
would be seen in all kinds of odd coloured garments, which
some of the people would be sure to give him at such times,
one side of his face would be shaved and the other not, or dis-

figured in some way with paint &c. He was a very remarkable man & much more might be written of his merry odd ways and drole tricks. he was the laughing stock of all who saw him.[43]

He is best remembered as the fool of the King Sutton Morrice Dancers. This troupe always came to Banbury for a few days at Whitsuntide, when Old Metal, in a queer, fanciful dress, with his staff, bladder and calf's tail, would keep the crowd at a distance, whilst his ready wit, grimaces, and marvellous powers of contortion kept crowds of grown-up people in roars of laughter. He was fond of appearing in different characters.[44]

"Old Mettle" also used to go with the morris dancers to the clubs, etc. I have seen him with the eight morris dancers in Banbury, all of them in their shirt sleeves, with bells tied by ribbons of all colours on their arms and legs, and wearing white trousers, "Mettle" acting as merryman to the lot, dressed in similar style, and with his face painted. They all danced and each had two white pocket handkerchiefs to whirl about in time with the music.[45]

The wit and jokes in use in the village [*Bloxham*] were of a simple nature, but did good service year after year, and always came up fresh. Probably a new set of jokes, and the disuse of the old ones, would have been resented by the audience. Village tradition tells of a famous "squire" who made a good deal of money by dancing. One of his most telling jokes (among a purely agricultural population) was that he knew plenty of bigger fools than himself, e g, those standing round him, for they worked for their living and he didn't.[46]

The Morris dancers were great in Bloxham until about 40 years ago. Charles Townsend and [*blank*] were in the last batch.
They were decked out pretty in Coventry ribbons + had bells on their legs. Besides the dancers were one who played the Tabor (a small drum) + piper 3 notes only: also the "Squire" a clown who made witty remarks and had a stick with a calf's tail at one end + a bullocks [*this word crossed out*] bladder blown out + having a handful of peas inside: he

asked riddles and knocked the boys with resounding bangs over the head with the bladder. Bloxham + Souldern danced against one another at the former place: the crowd was judge, + as may be imagined B won: tho' S had the best dancers B had the best clown + that took the people. Morris dancing took place at Whitsuntide.[47]

B– [*Bloxham*] was always noted for its Morris-dancers, and with a neighbouring village (S– [*Souldern*]) some six miles distant, enjoyed a local reputation. These villages danced against one-another at B– one evening in the early summer. The crowd were the judges, and, as may be surmised, B– won the match. For although the S– men danced better than their opponents, B– had the best "squire", + this took the people's fancy.[48]

John Barrett confirmed a/c. said [*morris*] was danced at "Statute" also. sometimes 8 of them. One Mettal was a great "fool" one of his jokes was that he knew a bigger fool than himself: naming someone", 'cause he works for his livin' + I don't."[49]

The horse-bells remind me of the morris-dancers. The countrymen used to practise their dancing at most of the villages, and at certain seasons of the year used to come into the town and go through their various dances, and then make a collection from the onlookers, and some of them were very clever at it. The men were dressed in their best, and wore white shirts with plaited sleeves and ribbons tied round their arms, and upon their legs were rows of small bells sewn upon strips of coloured leather. These bells were made in the same form as the horse-bells, that is to say they were of a round form with a slot in them, and a round shot to make them jingle as they danced. In size they were about as large as a marble, but the bells upon the horses were as large as a man's fist. In some of the morris-dances, each man carried a white stick about an inch in thickness and about eighteen inches in length, and this stick was used in their dances, sometimes tapping each other's stick together, and at other times one was held over the other's head, one dancer tapped his fellow-dancer with his stick, and at other times they would each have a white handkerchief and flourish in similar form. Their music was of a rude kind and known as the tabor and pipe. Their pipe was a one-handed flute with about four holes – three on the upper side for the fingers, and one underneath for the thumb. This was played with the left hand, and upon the little finger was held the tabor which was tapped by the right hand. The tabor was a small drum something like a tambourine. There was also a clown fantastically dressed who carried a long stick with a bladder at one end and calf's tail at the other for keeping off the boys, and sometimes he would have a handful of flour in his pocket, and if he found a boy very troublesome he used his flour with a handful in his face. This generally caused a laugh, and quieted him.[50]

1830
Mettle's last Parliamentary attempt was in 1830, when he was the opponent of Mr. Villiers Stuart. Although Mettle was never elected, he was quite sure to be chaired: and Mr. Heneage Legge will doubtless remember being chaired in Mettle's company, and how Mettle afterwards addressed him for it as "brother."[51]

Sunday, 22 August 1830
W Castle brought in by R Horseman for stealing a Watch from the house of W Smith Neithrop.[52]

Monday, 23 August to Thursday, 26 August 1830
[*Castle was locked up for a total of four nights.*[53]]

Thursday, 2 December 1830
William Castle Charles Gibbard & Pitcher brought by Thompson on charge of stealing Fowls from Mr James Golby.[54]

Friday, 3 December 1830
[*Castle was locked up for two nights.*[55]]

Saturday, 4 December 1830
Castle, Gibbard & Pitcher taken to Oxford.[56]

On one occasion, and, as far as we know, on one only, Mettle fell into deeper sorrow, and perhaps into crime. He was tried at Oxford on a charge of being concerned, with others, in a burglary at Neithrop: he tried playing the fool in Court, in order to get off, and made most ugly faces at the Judge; but it wouldn't do there – he was found guilty, and sentenced to be hanged, at which Mettle grinned worse than before. But here fortune favoured him at last, for a petition from his Banbury friends shewed him to be generally considered an idiot, and then he received a pardon.[57]

About 20 years since he was tried, in company with others at Oxford, for a burglary at Neithrop, and sentenced to die, but was pardoned on the petition of persons who had long known him, and who believed he had been the dupe of designing men.[58]

He was a parishioner of Neithrop, in which place he gained a settlement by sleeping in an old boat, moored by the side of the canal: many amusing circumstances were related at a trial, when Neithrop was saddled with the charge of him.[59]

Tuesday, 7 June 1831
W Castle & William Hall brought by D Claridge Charged with breaking open a House at Shutford.[60]

Wednesday, 8 June 1831
Castle & Hall taken to Broughton & Committed to Oxford by Mr Wyatt.[61]

[*Castle was locked up for two nights.*[62]]

Thursday, 9 June 1831
Castle & Hall taken to Oxford by D Claridge on the Coach at 3 O Clock.[63]

OXFORD. *Commitments to our County Gaol* ... James Hall and William Castle, charged with breaking open the dwelling house of Isaac Smith, at Shutford East, and stealing therefrom a gold watch, &c.[64]

Monday, 3 October 1831
Robert Griffin of Shutford brought by D Claridge charged with being with Castle & Hall at the Robbery at Shutford.[65]

After July 1832
His favourite trade of aping the fool did not serve him always;

his match trade was but precarious, and when the Reform Bill did away with Mettle's popularity, by giving *votes* to his supporters, they pitifully turned their backs upon him, and set up Tancred instead. In his state of almost destitution, *Saturday*, with its *emptied pantries*, was his best friend. He gained a settlement in Neithrop township by sleeping in an old boat that was moored by the side of the canal.[66]

1834
The New Poor-Law was as bad a blow to Mettle as was the Reform Bill; but to send Mettle to the Poor-house would have annihilated all the then popularity of the Whigs – worse than sending Frost to Tasman's Peninsula, or Richard Oastler to the Fleet – and therefore some out-door relief was obtained for him.[67]

Tuesday, 21 April 1835
William Castle alias Mettle brought from the Cage by R Butler on Charge of breaking Mr Grimbly's Windows.[68]

[*Castle does not appear to have been locked up overnight for this offence, but see below for his punishment.*]

Thursday, 23 April 1835
Metal taken to the Office & Ordered to sit in the stocks 4 hours.[69]

Tuesday, 30 May 1837
The other instance of Mettle's gravity was when his mother died. The poor fellow, who was a diligent church-goer, thought it right on that occasion to appear like other people; so he begged a common hat, a common coat, waistcoat, and trousers, all of rusty black, with a white shirt, and, for a time, looked almost like a gentleman.[70]

[*Anne Castle, living at the time of her death at Adderbury West, was buried in Adderbury churchyard on Tuesday, 30 May 1837, aged 74.*]

Sunday, 4 June 1837
When she died, he succeeded in getting, from one quarter or another, a decent suit of black, and a white shirt, and we

recollect seeing him on the following Sunday, returning from Church, for the first time dressed like other people.[71]

Probably Friday, 9 April 1841

He had had two fits previously; and had complained of a pain in his head ever since our last fair, when someone tripped up his heels, and he fell heavily on the back of his head.[72]

May 1841

THE NEW CANDIDATE. – In our last number we promised that if the Tories of Banbury remained for another week destitute of a candidate, we would direct them to one: but as it appeared by the *Oxfordshire Herald* of the same date that they had been successful, and that Mr. W. Metal (erroneously spelt "Mettle" in the Herald) was to oppose Mr. Tancred, on the Tory interest, we did not suppose that we should be called upon to redeem our pledge. Still as the sudden death of the man of their choice (fortune will surely never weary of persecuting them) must have altogether deranged them of their plans, we feel bound in honour to give them some assistance, especially as we have always desired that they should start the best man they could get. There are those of the party who must have felt some doubt of the propriety of supporting Metal, because the speech delivered by him, as quoted in the Herald, shews that he was an advocate for untaxed food, of which most Tories have a greater horror than they have of the starvation of their fellow creatures, and therefore whatever might have been the exertions of the subdistributor of stamps at Banbury, and Mr. Metal's other personal friends and admirers, who from attachment to the individuals might have waived some of their opinions, still he could hardly, from the cause above stated, been generally acceptable to their party.[73]

[*This is a satirical response to the piece quoted in the 1818 section, above.*]

Tuesday, 1 June 1841

On the preceding evening he had, in the vocation of fool, accompanied a party of Morris Dancers round Banbury, and seemed, and no doubt felt, in as high glee as he had ever been.[74]

No longer ago than Tuesday sen-night Mettle was as merry as Whitsuntide could make him, parading the streets of Banbury with a troop of morris-dancers.[75]

Wednesday, 2 June 1841
The following morning, while mending his patchwork dress, with the intention of going to Adderbury Club, he fell from his seat and expired instantly.[76]

On Wednesday morning he got up, and began to mend his patchwork that he might go to Adderbury club. He had rested at a lodging-house kept by Mrs. Thorp, and, as he sat by the grate, was also nursing Mrs. T.'s infant. Suddenly he said to a little girl who was in the room – "*Take the babby*;" and then immediately fell against the grate, the little girl, afraid, fetched her mother; the poor fellow ruttled a little in his throat; the woman sent for the doctor, but before that aid could arrive Mettle was quite dead. A jury sat, and returned a verdict of "Death from apoplexy."[77]

His age was 52 or 53. The surgeon who made the post mortem examination stated, that on opening the head, he found that the death had been caused by an effusion of blood upon the brain, which had probably been accelerated by the exertions which the deceased had used on the preceding day, when in attendance upon the morris dancers.[78]

His "household effects," which consist of a heap of straw, a pocket-knife, a stool, and a table, fall (we suppose) into the hands of the parish authorities.[79]

Friday, 4 June 1841
[*William Castle was buried in Banbury on Friday, 4 June 1841. In the burial register entry his age was given as 52, and his place of habitation at the time of death as Grimsbury.*]

Notes
I am grateful for the assistance of Malcolm Graham and his staff at the Centre For Oxfordshire Studies, Oxford Library; Simon Townsend (Senior Museum Officer) and Chris Kelly (Assistant Curator) at Banbury Museum; Martin Allett at the Centre For Banburyshire Studies, Banbury Library; Malcolm Taylor (Librarian), Vaughan Williams Memorial Library, Cecil Sharp House, London; Vera Wood.

1. William Potts MSS., Banbury Museum, Box 28; 990,71,481, typescript of a letter to Mr [Thomas Ward] Boss, from G. Barrett, St Kilda, Vic [sic], 16/17 May 1904, 8.
2. *Oxford University, City, and County Herald*, 12 June 1841, p. 4.
3. *The Guardian* [Banbury], 5 June 1841, p. 4. Also in *Oxford Chronicle*, 4 June 1841, p. 4 with identical text.
4. *Oxford University, City, and County Herald*, 12 June 1841, p. 4.
5. Janet Heatley Blunt MSS., Vaughan Williams Memorial Library, Cecil Sharp House, London. Vol. XIX, letter to Cecil Sharp, 1 May 1922.
6. George Herbert, *Shoemaker's Window: Recollections of a Midland Town before the Railway Age*, ed. Christiana S. Cheney (Oxford: Blackwell, 1949), pp. xi–xii. Herbert's original handwritten manuscript consists of 190 foolscap pages, written as a series of letters to friends circa 1898 to 1900. He died 21 December, 1902.
7. *Oxford University, City, and County Herald*, 12 June 1841, p. 4.
8. Unlocated 1841 newspaper cutting, pasted on the rear of the painting in Banbury Museum. Transcribed in Russell Wortley MSS, National Centre for English Cultural Tradition and Language, University of Sheffield, G III 5g.
9. *Oxford University, City, and County Herald*, 12 June 1841, p. 4.
10. *The Guardian* [Banbury], 5 June 1841, p. 4. Also in *Oxford Chronicle*, 4 June 1841, p. 4 with identical text.
11. Potts MSS.
12. *Oxford University, City, and County Herald*, 12 June 1841, p. 4.
13. *Oxford University, City, and County Herald*, 29 May 1841, p. 2.
14. *The Guardian* [Banbury], 5 June 1841, p. 4. Also in *Oxford Chronicle*, 4 June 1841, p. 4 with identical text.
15. *Oxford University, City, and County Herald*, 12 June 1841, p. 4.
16. William Potts, *A History of Banbury* (Banbury: Banbury Guardian, 1958), pp. 203–4. Potts was born in 1868, and thus had no first hand knowledge of Castle. His sources for the election riot include a series of scrapbooks in Banbury Borough Museum (these are apparently no longer in the archive), containing information from Superintendent W. Thompson and Mr W. Dickason, which he acknowledges, and Sarah Beesley's *My life* (n.p. [Banbury]: 'Printed for private circulation,' n.d. [1892]). Sarah Beesley was born Sarah Rusher in Banbury in March 1812.
17. *Oxford University, City, and County Herald*, 12 June 1841, p. 4.
18. *Jackson's Oxford Journal*, 18 March 1820, p. 3.
19. Beesley, *My life*, pp. 18–19.
20. Potts, *A History of Banbury*, pp. 203–4.
21. Herbert, *Shoemaker's Window*, p. 8.
22. *Ibid.*, p. 41, fn. 1.
23. *Oxford University, City, and County Herald*, 12 June 1841, p. 4.
24. *Jackson's Oxford Journal*, 17 June 1826, p. 4.
25. *Oxford University, City, and County Herald*, 12 June 1841, p. 4.
26. Herbert, *Shoemaker's Window*, pp. 113-14.
27. *Ibid.*, p. 114, fn. by the editor, written 1948.
28. Thomas Ward Boss, *Reminiscences of Old Banbury*, (1903), p. 24. Boss was born in 1825, and lived for his first seven years in Oxford, before moving to Banbury.
29. Beesley, *My life*, pp. 14–15.
30. *Oxford University, City, and County Herald*, 12 June 1841, p. 4.
31. William Potts MSS., Banbury Museum, Box 28; 990,71,481, typescript of a letter to Mr [Thomas Ward] Boss, from G. Barrett, St Kilda, Vic [sic], 16/17 May

1904, 8.

32. Janet Heatley Blunt MSS., Vaughan Williams Memorial Library, Cecil Sharp House, London. Vol. XIX, letter to Cecil Sharp, 1 May 1922.

33. A single sheet of handwritten text —undated, but apparently nineteenth century – slipped into the rear frame alcove of the painting which hangs in Banbury Museum.

34. Herbert, *Shoemaker's Window*, p. 9.

35. *The Guardian* [Banbury], 5 June 1841, p. 4. Also in *Oxford Chronicle*, 4 June 1841, p. 4 with identical text.

36. *Oxford University, City, and County Herald*, 12 June 1841, p. 4.

37. *Ibid*.

38. Herbert, *Shoemaker's Window*, p. 9.

39. *Ibid*.

40. *The Guardian* [Banbury], 5 June 1841, p. 4. Also in *Oxford Chronicle*, 4 June 1841, p. 4 with identical text.

41. William Potts MSS. Box 28; 990,71,329, commercial exercise book, f. 11½. Legend [on f.1] 'Some Reccolections [*sic*] of Old Banburie over 60 years ago No 1 and Experiences and thoughts by an old Banbury'.

42. Blunt MSS.

43. Single sheet of handwritten text, Banbury Museum.

44. Boss, *Reminiscences of Old Banbury*, p. 24.

45. Beasley, *My life*, p. 15.

46. O. V. Aplin collection, Oxfordshire Archives. Apl. III/iii/3, notes for a proposed lecture entitled 'A vanished Custom,' written circa 1894.

47. *Ibid*.

48. *Ibid*.

49. *Ibid*, Apl III/iii/18, f.1v, dated 19 April 1894.

50. Herbert, *Shoemaker's Window*, p. 119.

51. *Oxford University, City, and County Herald*, 12 June 1841, p. 4.

52. P. Renold, ed., *Banbury Gaol Records* (Banbury: Banbury Historical Society, 1987), p. 5.

53. *Ibid*., p. 51.

54. *Ibid*., p. 6.

55. *Ibid*., p. 51.

56. *Ibid*., p. 6.

57. *Oxford University, City, and County Herald*, 12 June 1841, p. 4.

58. *The Guardian* [Banbury], 5 June 1841, p. 4. Also in *Oxford Chronicle*, 4 June 1841, p. 4 with identical text.

59. *Ibid*.

60. Renold, *Banbury Gaol Records*, p. 10.

61. *Ibid*.

62. *Ibid*., p. 52.

63. *Ibid*., p. 10.

64. *Jackson's Oxford Journal*, 11 June 1831, p. 3.

65. Renold, *Banbury Gaol Records*, p. 11.

66. *Oxford University, City, and County Herald*, 12 June 1841, p. 4.

67. *Ibid*.

68. Renold, *Banbury Gaol Records*, p. 35.

69. *Ibid*.

70. *Oxford University, City, and County Herald*, 12 June 1841, p. 4.

71. *The Guardian* [Banbury], 5 June 1841, p. 4. Also in *Oxford Chronicle*, 4 June 1841, p. 4 with identical text.

72. Unlocated 1841 newspaper cutting, Wortley MSS.
73. *Oxford Chronicle*, 5 June 1841, p. 4.
74. *The Guardian* [Banbury], 5 June 1841, p. 4. Also in *Oxford Chronicle*, 4 June 1841, p. 4 with identical text.
75. *Oxford University, City, and County Herald*, 12 June 1841, p. 4.
76. *The Guardian* [Banbury], 5 June 1841, p. 4. Also in *Oxford Chronicle*, 4 June 1841, p. 4 with identical text.
77. *Oxford University, City, and County Herald*, 12 June 1841, p. 4.
78. Unlocated 1841 newspaper cutting, Wortley MSS.
79. *Oxford University, City, and County Herald*, 12 June 1841, p. 4.

Further reading

Chandler, Keith. *'Ribbons, Bells and Squeaking Fiddles'. The Social History of Morris Dancing in the English South Midlands, 1660–1900*. Enfield Lock: Hisarlik Press, for the Folklore Society, 1993.

Chandler, Keith. *Morris Dancing in the English South Midlands, 1660–1900. A Chronological Gazetteer*. Enfield Lock: Hisarlik Press, for the Folklore Society, 1993.

The above two volumes are also available in updated form on CD ROM format from Musical Traditions (www.mustrad.org.uk).

G.A.S.   *Page 27*
'The eight dancers formed stars in the centre.'
Frontispiece.

Illustration by Elsie Anna Wood from *Girls of the Abbey
School* by Elsie J Oxenham.

Meeting the prophet: Cecil Sharp and the English folk revival as seen by Elsie J. Oxenham

Allison Thompson

Introduction

There are now no dancers living who can boast of having been taught directly by Cecil Sharp himself, or who experienced at first hand the heady and exciting days of the pre-war folk revival when the romantic vision of a resurrected Merrie Olde Englande bumped heads with the suffragists' war for the vote, when gentlemen in white tie at elegant parties stumbled through sword dances with umbrellas and walking sticks, and when Sharp and his followers believed that by giving folk dances and songs back to the wretched working poor, one could raise their spirits and their spirituality out of the muck and into an aesthetic appreciation that would make their working lives healthier (and more productive). Like the gas-lamps that illumined it, that world is now so far removed from us that many of its beliefs and aspirations are hard to comprehend. Fortunately, the spirit of this early English folk revival found an inspiring and popular chronicler in Elsie J Oxenham, author of ninety books for schoolgirls and young women. In her forty-volume 'Abbey Girls' series, she provided her readers with a clear view of some of Sharp's principles and practices, permitting us to obtain a better understanding of the romantic fervour that fuelled the folk revival in both England and the United States.

Starting with the first book, *The Girls of the Hamlet Club* (1914), the Abbey Girls series incorporated a love of nature and beauty, a veiled but ever-present religious outlook, youthful characters and interests and a little romance along with English folk dance. Though Oxenham never mentioned the English Folk Dance Society or its leaders and teachers by name, keeping firmly to her invented nicknames, several of her early novels feature vignettes of Cecil Sharp, Douglas Kennedy (late Director of the English Folk Dance & Song Society) and his sister, Helen Kennedy North, May Gadd (late Director of the Country Dance & Song Society of America), D.C. Daking and other teachers of the early revival movement.

Some of Oxenham's descriptions and comments are detailed enough to provide us with important information about the early days of the folk revival: the range of dances in the repertoire; methods of teaching country dances; character sketches of Sharp and some of his teachers; details of certain dances that may be discarded or glossed over today; and the attitudes of devotees towards dancing. Oxenham was a writer who drew heavily and meticulously from life: her descriptions of landscapes, for example, are readily identifiable today. For this reason, her descriptions of the people involved in the early English folk dance revival take on a certain authority. In addition to their importance as a rose-coloured window into the folk revival, we should note that Oxenham's novels were read eagerly as each one appeared, and were instrumental in stimulating many readers' curiosity about dancing.[1] Her works continue to command a devoted following.

Elsie J. Oxenham

Elsie Jeanette Dunkerley was born in Southport, Lancashire, in 1880, the first child in a family of four girls and two boys. In 1882, the family moved to London, where Elsie spent the first half of her life, attending private schools. Elsie grew up in a literary and religious atmosphere. Her father, William Dunkerley, was a prolific novelist who wrote under the pseudonym John Oxenham. Known to the literary world simply as J.O., he wrote adventure stories as well as sentimental and mystical novels. Elsie, her sister Erica and the two boys all adopted the name Oxenham for their own writing. Elsie's first book, *Goblin Island*, appeared in 1907 and was followed by sixteen more until *The Abbey Girls* (1920) returned to the characters and folk-dance setting of *The Girls of the Hamlet Club* (1914) and launched the first of the several series that Oxenham wrote for girls.

It is still not known for certain when or how Oxenham discovered the English Folk Dance Society (formed by Cecil Sharp and others in late 1911), but it is believed to be perhaps as early as 1912, when Oxenham would have been in her early thirties. Because of the differences in the way she wrote about dancing in her first and in her second folk-dance book, a persuasive argument has been made that at the time of her earliest folk-dance book (1914), Oxenham was a spectator, possibly of performances by Mary Neal's Esperance Society girls, but that by 1919 or 1920 she had herself become a dancer and attended one of the Cheltenham summer schools organised by Cecil Sharp.[2] Because several of her books include characters who are shy and awkward writers transformed by folk dancing into more confident and expressive people, it is often assumed that this was Oxenham's personal experience. Oxenham and her family moved from London to Sussex in 1922 and she continued with some sort of undocumented dance or dance teaching for some years until doctors advised her to stop. She was able, for example, to describe with accuracy and detail the style and method of teaching of dances from *The Apted Book* (edited and published by the Heffners in the late-1930s). Oxenham never married. She died on 9 January 1960.[3]

The Abbey Girls

Oxenham's principal goal with her Abbey Girls series was not, in fact, to document the English folk revival: she was simply telling the stories of the characters she loved. The Abbey Girls series is difficult to summarise, given that it comprises forty-plus novels, was written over a forty-year time span and has an interrelated and often confusing cast of characters. The books feature girls who are attending, or who have attended, the imaginary Abbey School in Buckinghamshire, near the Oxfordshire border. Today, the books are generally lumped into the genre 'school stories'. But Oxenham's themes differ from those of standard school stories, especially those written for boys, such as Rudyard

Kipling's *Stalky & Co*. (1899) or P.G. Wodehouse's *The White Feather* (1907). Oxenham's stories do not address typical boys' school story topics such as thrilling school matches, bullying prefects or teachers, or misunderstood cases of cowardice, cheating or theft. Her tales rarely pit one girl against another, the teachers or a group of girls; they are more often about how a girl finds satisfaction in resolving conflict and helping others, or how she finds the artistic outlet she needs through music or education, usually introduced to her by one or more of the Abbey girls through the medium of folk dance

The Abbey Girls series gets its name from the imaginary, ruined Cistercian Abbey of Gracedieu, located near the school. The two principal Abbey Girls, Joan and Joy Shirley, cousins who look almost identical, are initially too poor to attend the school. However, in *The Abbey Girls* (1920), Joy's wealthy, estranged grandfather wills the Abbey, to the better (that is, the more thoughtful, mature and caring) girl, Joan, while to Joy he gives the adjacent manor house. The girls attend the school, eventually becoming the fourth and fifth May Queens,[4] respectively, and make many friends, particularly Jen, Rosamund and Maidlin, whose stories become intertwined with theirs.

The Abbey Girls novels encourage moral, aesthetic and religious sensibilities. Girls frequently encourage each other to 'do the straight thing', or are disapproving of any girl who has 'funked her duty'. In some stories the 'spirit' of the Abbey – the attributes of friendliness, courage, generosity and self-sacrifice – is explicitly discussed as a spirit that all the girls, brought together first by their love of folk dancing, develop. Elsewhere, the theory of duty is discussed: in one tale, thoughtful Mary proposes while everyone has her own occupation (from lady of the manor to being housekeeper or cook to having babies) everyone also has something extra that they can contribute, such as Guiding, or teaching Sunday School classes.

Throughout her books, Oxenham's characters express a common aesthetic: a love of nature and the English countryside; a love of beautiful, handmade things (true to the spirit of the Arts-and-Crafts Movement, the wealthy Joy eventually supports a village pottery, a weaving school, basket-work and lace-making factories, a girls' hostel and a babies' home) and, of course, the love of music and dance. Ironically, it is clear from oblique remarks that Oxenham was aware of the fact that it takes money to buy Liberty frocks and expensive hand-made pottery – but she chose to ignore this dilemma. Her rich girls are very generous to the poor ones, and that seems to take care of the issue.

A strong sense of social class pervades the novels. As in many nineteenth-century novels, the dislikeable girls are those whose fathers have made their money from trade (as opposed to having inherited land and its responsibilities), or those who are showy and brag, or who 'put on side'. The good girls, by contrast, work hard for scholarships, but may give them up in favour of deserving friends or relatives, or chuck them at great personal sacrifice so they can stay home to help their widowed mothers with the little ones, and so on. The admired girls, no matter how poor, are almost always 'gentle-women', in a way that the village girls or the Women's Institute members are not. Thus, the responses of Oxenham's characters to the aesthetics of dance are often based on their class: the nouveaux-riche girls don't appreciate it; the lower classes enjoy it but must be trained to do it right; it is the mid-dle to upper-class girls who really thrill to its artistry.

For Oxenham's novels – like all romances, whether set in schools or not – are profoundly conservative in a late Victorian way. The principal Abbey girls marry well, even brilliantly: men who are rich, titled, usually land-owners (an important nineteenth-century criterion) or, if not land-own-ers, at least famous and talented, usually musically. The girls' interactions with the world reinforce this nineteenth-century hierarchy. They are pleasant, kind and helpful to poor girls and the lower orders – but woe betide anyone who gets a bit 'out of her place' – such as as when the grown-up Carrie – a trouble-maker both at school and later as an adult – attempts to call Joy, Lady Marchwood, by her first name. She is royally and firmly squashed.

How does English folk dancing support the expression of Oxenham's sensibilities? First, Oxenham clearly found that the communal nature of folk dancing fitted in with her phi-losophy of teamwork and fair play. Thus, in 1923 she charac-terised folk dancers as 'ordinary jolly people, who love to have a good time and who don't swank or put on side, and who aren't any of them a scrap affected, *or they couldn't do those dances!*'[5] [emphasis added]

Pleasure in dancing can even transcend cultural barriers: a philosophy that Oxenham made most concrete in *Jen of the Abbey School* (1927),[6] in which Jen, living in Yorkshire with her invalid father, teaches folk dancing to the children of the village as well as the children of the navvies brought in to build a big dam and who live in the temporary 'Tin Town'. The two groups have regarded each other with active dislike, but Jen cunningly suggests that the children give a show and then points out that neither group is large enough to ensure success alone. The children and their parents are thus brought together, as Jen tells a visitor:

> "This dancing is doing a big thing! .... Little village kids dancing with little Tin Town! Big village fellows in a morris side with Tin Town chaps! Big girls from Tin Town partners with big boys from the village! And all the parents of both sets looking on, all as happy as they can be! [*Jen then adds a phrase repeated often in the canon*] I always think that in real folk-dancing you enjoy yourself so much that you've simply no time for thinking about yourself."[7]

However, while folk dancing can lower class barriers in certain carefully defined situations, in general the country dancing woven throughout the Abbey Girl series works to reinforce the social conservatism of Oxenham's (and Sharp's) world. Oxenham and Sharp both came from well-to-do, artistic, though not quite 'country house', backgrounds. Oxenham's clearly expressed, Edwardian attitudes towards class, typical of the period, were no doubt part of the reason why Cecil Sharp chose to use 'the right sort'– upper-middle-class young people such as Douglas and Helen Kennedy and Maud and Helen Karpeles, George Butterworth and Perceval Lucas, as members of his demonstration team and teaching staff. This decision 'to use the well-bred young women and men who could afford to do 'something honorary and useful' as his associates gave his work a status which [his organisational rival Mary] Neal's combination of seamstresses and suffragettes could not hope to emulate'[8] and contributed to his success with the moneyed establishment. Whether Sharp was ever aware of Oxenham's work – or grateful to her – her writings which so firmly rooted her dancing girls in the idyl-

lic upper-class countryside certainly helped to reinforce the
social cachet of Sharp's organisation.

Thus, from the springboard of Oxenham's fictional coun-
try-house world, she showed her young readers that folk-
dancing was a respectable, safe and pretty way for the classes
to mix, albeit in a carefully controlled environment, such as
the Whitsun fete described at length in *The Abbey Girls Play
Up*. Here the Abbey Girls are providing the bounty – the
music, the art – and they are serving the people, but only by
resurrecting old folkways, not by training them for the urban
future. For, after all, what could be more conservative than
the picture of the happy villagers dancing around the
Maypole under the benevolent but firm eye of the presiding
gentry?

In fact, the real 'folk' are conspicuously absent from the
enchanting Abbey Girl world: the world of the pretty girls,
the beautiful Abbey, nature, babies, dance and music. With
the single exception of Jen's cook in Yorkshire, who takes her
to see her village's performance of a sword dance at
Christmas (the kit described is clearly that of the traditional
team of the village of Handsworth, and the detail of the excellent and inspiring description makes one certain that
Oxenham saw a performance first-hand), the girls neither
have nor seek out original sources of inspiration in their
hobby. No kindly old retainer sings to them; neither do they
canvass the villages for morris or country dancing remnants.
The dance classes that the girls hold for the Women's
Institutes are both a pleasure and a duty, but few of the village
women become even 'competent', let alone 'keen'. This
myopia was probably due in part to Oxenham's own personal
predilections, since she drew so heavily from life. Although
she taught dancing to her Camp Fire for some years prior to
1922 (learning, one presumes, wrongly from books, as her
character Cicely does), she was primarily a London-based
dancer, not a collector. Oxenham's blindness to the presence
of the real 'folk' may also reflect the degree of control that
Cecil Sharp kept over his material and the collection process
in general, since he explicitly discouraged collection by anyone outside his circle.[9]

Folk dance also worked for Oxenham as a means of under-
scoring plot and character issues. Take, for example the short
story 'Honour Your Partner', which appeared in *The British*

Girl's Annual of 1922. Two best friends have quarrelled and won't dance as partners as they normally do. Their school enters a inter-school competition with a sword dance, the Flamborough, but after the first class, the teacher sprains her ankle and cannot teach. A new, younger girl, who idolises the two quarrelling girls, and who attended Sharp's Summer School at Cheltenham but is to shy to mention it, knows she could teach the dance – after all, at Cheltenham, one had to learn every position in the dance. For the good of the school, she swallows her shyness, leads the team of older girls to victory and, by clever placement of the two quarrelling friends (they are dancers eight and three and must work together for the 'threedling'), heals the breach. Oxenham's skill is such that the dances or even the specific movements like threedling are not described in a static fashion – in fact, she does not describe them at all. Instead, she illuminates the relationships between the girls – first quarrelling, then becoming friends again through the movements of the dances. This matter-of-fact incorporation of dance into the very fabric of ordinary life separates Oxenham from any other writer about dance.

For Oxenham writes movingly about the beauty of dance, and her characters express feelings about or reactions to the dance in a way that modern dancers can easily identify with. When Cicely, a principal character in the first few books, finally sees men dancers (that is, not school girls) demonstrate a morris dance, she is moved almost to tears. A friend analyses her response as coming 'face to face with beauty unexpectedly – beauty that you could see. Some people find it in music and some in books ... You realised it in movement today, through a thing you loved already ...'[10] Such passionate descriptions of dance and music remain appealing today.

Finally, in some of Oxenham's novels, folk dancing is seen as having almost a spiritually redemptive effect. Its wholesomeness and naturalness 'save' several characters, or are offered as a general panacea for poor posture, shyness or even mental imbalance. For example, Jen tells Mary (herself saved by dancing from her 'unhealthy daydreams') to help another shy girl who has an unhealthy crush on Mary by getting her to folk dance. 'If there's one thing that teaches balance and control, it's country-dancing. Get it into her feet and body, and you may get it into her mind too. Make her come to classes and bully her into common sense!"[11] Here, balance and control are metaphors for a fully integrated personality, as well as representing the physical skills needed for good dancing.

The Prophet and his acolytes

While folk-dancing is at least mentioned in all the books, in a few stories in the canon, notably *The New Abbey Girls* (1923), *The Abbey Girls Go Back To School* (1922), set at the Folk Dance Summer School in Cheltenham, and *The Abbey Girls In Town* (1925), set at the Christmas school at the Chelsea Polytechnic Institute in London, the dancing forms a key plot element and provides us as well with the clearest information about Sharp and his teachers. These books provide us with interesting character vignettes of the people Oxenham adored. In addition, they give us insights into the prevailing style of teaching and the 'certification' process, and, finally, a visceral sense of the era that perceived these dances both as peculiarly and representationally English and as a panacea for the ills of modern society.

Cecil Sharp appears in these early books as, varyingly, 'The Director' or 'The Prophet': the latter name particularly for his role, as both he and Oxenham viewed it, in saving dances and customs about to die.[12] Thus, in the following lengthy selection, we enjoy seeing Sharp and his Christmas School (set in 'Abbey Time' c.1919 or 1920) through the eyes of Ruth, a South African girl, who is visiting her cousins and the Abbey Girls for the first time:

> The big gym. of the Chelsea Polytechnic was even more of an ant-heap than the dressing-rooms, and a very much disturbed ant-heap at that. The whole six hundred students were gathered there, all excited, all happy, all looking for friends or greeting them eagerly ... Girls hung over the edge of the gallery to wave to friends just discovered below; girls on the window-sills called greetings to others who had climbed up on the ladders and bars of the gymnastic apparatus; girls ran about looking for chairs or song-books. Some one began to clap, and the hall rang with the welcome of six hundred folk-dancers to their chief. The white-haired Director appeared on the platform and

A.G.B.S.   *Page* 180.
' To the music of Karen's fiddle, they danced on the turf.'

Illustration by Elsie Anna Wood from *Abbey Girls Go Back to School* by Elsie J Oxenham.

smiling acknowledged the greeting. He struck a chord on the piano, and silence fell; he announced, "Number One," and began to play a rippling accompaniment.

"*How they sing!*" Ruth murmured. "Oh, I love this part of it! And what pretty songs! And how beautifully he accompanies! ..."

The half-hour's singing was all too short. The Director gave out a few notices, and particularly cautioned newcomers against too hard work in the first few days – "I say this at every School, but nobody ever listens to me!"

"Old dear!" Joy murmured. "He does try to take care of us! Who minds being a little stiff to-morrow?"

[*Then there are morris dance demonstrations: the women dance Laudnum Bunches (handkerchiefs); the men, Adderbury Constant Billy (sticks).*]

"I could go on watching this for ever!" Ruth murmured at the end. "But I'm sure they couldn't go on dancing for ever! I never saw anything more exciting in my life! But fancy dancing being so thrilling!"

"It's so full of life and strength and meaning," Mary said soberly. "We saw a lot of it last summer, at the week's festival. It's very English; you wouldn't expect us to have evolved a dreamy or a stately dance, as France or Spain might do."[13]

In appearances like this and the following one, Sharp is represented as a kindly old man, urging the students to rest or asking them to wear afternoon frocks rather than gym tunics to the afternoon classes:

The Pixie's eyes were following the Director as he made his way to the piano. "Don't you love to watch him at these schools? He looks so happy! As if he were enjoying himself as much as anybody. And I love the way he goes round the rooms, just to see that we're all happy too! ... I do think he goes about looking like a happy uncle or grandfather."[14]

Or again, when the entire summer school dances the last dance together, Sellenger's Round: '...the whole party, of several hundred, were massed in great rings, one inside the other, all revolving in alternate directions, the loved Prophet in the centre, smiling even more happily than usual.'[15] Joshua (Douglas Kennedy) arranges the rings, telling each one which way to slip in the first figure, and watching as they dance with their arms rising up in the second figure like disciples honouring their master.

As other studies have revealed, however, Sharp had a dictatorial side: he knew that he was right, that his organisation was right and that his teachers/disciples were right. Oxenham unconsciously documents his beliefs when she depicts the teaching style of Sharp's disciples, as well as in the following incident in which we see Sharp himself. Here, a sympathetic teacher (the Pixie) saves the intermediate group from Sharp's critique of their performance of Hunsdon House, challenging because of its slow tempo, which requires sensitive and artistic dancing. One girl tells her friends that:

> We were attempting 'Hunsdon House,' and you know the Director's feeling for 'Hunsdon House!' We were *not* doing it well; and suddenly he walked in! We nearly died with horror at the thought of him watching us. But she [the Pixie] knew! She told him we were just beginning it, and then she said it would be such a treat to us if he would just play it for us! The pianist jumped up, only too delighted, I'm sure, after what he said about 'Hunsdon House' in his lecture on accompanying the other day; and he sat down and played it perfectly for us. But the point was that he'd got his back to us! We could have hugged her! Then he went off, quite happy; and we felt we'd escaped, so we were quite happy ...[16]

Sharp and his teachers were very firm about there being only one right way to perform and that they alone knew it. For example, a tenet that Cecil Sharp held strongly, as good franchise-owners do, was the importance of learning from his trained teachers, rather than from books. Oxenham faithfully records this precept for us in several of the early books. For example, in *The Abbey Girls Go Back To School*, the strong-willed Cicely discovers that, relying on books to guide her, she has been teaching her friends bad style. She comes in for some heavy criticism from 'Madam' (Helen Kennedy North), but her eagerness to atone and her courage to go back to tell her friends that she was wrong win Madam's respect and, eventually, her friendship. It has been suggested that Cicely's experience was Oxenham's own, since she taught dancing to her Camp Fire[17] from 1916 to 1922, and it would appear from inference that she attended at least one of the three summer schools held at Cheltenham in 1920, 1921 and 1922.

As further evidence of Sharp's strong hand on style and content in the early revival movement, an element that emerges clearly in Oxenham's picture of this period is the outright bossiness of the teachers, from the little girls teaching each other to the style of Madam. Today, many teachers of English country dance try to minimise the number of commands and corrections that they give and emphasise instead the social element of dance. Note instead young Jansy's orders and forthright criticisms as she teaches Rufty Tufty to three other girls, dancing, as they often do, out-of-doors to the singing of one girl:

> "Siding – oh, you'll have to practice that! Set to your partner. Now go to your own wall – put your hand across you, Lindy; you're being a woman. Now give your right hand to me; I'm a man – your *right*, I said! ... Now I want to see that again. Be careful of your setting! Margaret sometimes puts one toe in front of the other; she mustn't do it – it's wrong. Remember what hand to use when you lead out; left the first time and back with the right; then the other way round."[18]

Two of Sharp's teachers make important appearances in the Oxenham canon; indeed, *The Abbey Girls Go Back To School* is dedicated to them 'with thanks for all they have given to me': Helen Kennedy North and D.C. 'Daisie' Daking. Oxenham characterised Helen Kennedy North as 'Madam', 'Duchess', or 'She Who Must Be Obeyed', describing her as 'big and fair and jolly, with a very emphatic air of authority, and eyes which missed nothing'. Madam's graceful posture and beautiful dancing are commented on several times with admiration. But Madam is tough with her students. Note Madam's style as described by Cicely, the President of the Hamlet Club:

> ... I could understand people being scared of her
> ... This is Madam, at the end of a dance, when
> she's really worked up! "I *won't* have it! You *dread-*
> *ful* people! Not *one* of you ever listens to a *word* I
> say! I don't know how people *can* be so stupid! You
> haven't *danced* for me *once* yet all this week! Go
> right back to the beginning and do the whole
> dance over again; and do think what you're doing.
> You simply don't use your brains at all! You have
> the most complicated sort of minds! If there is a
> difficult or awkward way to do a thing, you invari-
> ably choose it! Now try to show me a *dance*, for
> once!"[19]

By contrast, Daking, petite, vibrant and more approach-able, is characterised as 'the Pixie'. 'She's a lovely dancer, too' says one girl. 'Fair hair – glasses – bright quick blue eyes – every bit as bossy as Madam, though she's such a dot ...'[20] The Pixie calls morris handkerchiefs 'wavies' and the inactives, 'the dud couple' and asks people to do it again, 'for luck'. Of greater interest, perhaps, are Oxenham's descriptions (which tally faithfully with other accounts) of Daking's activities in teaching dance to the soldiers of World War One, described in admiring detail. The Pixie was behind the lines in France and Germany, where she is mentioned as teaching the Flamborough and Kirkby Malzeard sword dances, a little morris and 'Galopede', 'Newcastle' and 'The Butterfly'.

> We took the men when they came out of hospital,
> not fit to go back into the line, and with no spirit
> for it, with the terrible disappointment still on
> them of not having been sent back to England.
> They hadn't been home and seen their friends,
> and they had no heart to take up the fight again.
> They weren't in a state to be drilled and made fit.
> Through dancing and music we gave them new
> life, new interest, courage to begin anew. *Then* the
> physical training people could do something with
> them. And that is something folk-dancing did for
> our country during the war.[21]

Douglas Kennedy, the future Director of the EFDSS, May Gadd, the future Director of the CDSS, and Maud Karpeles, Sharp's principal biographer, also make cameo appearances in the London-based Abbey Girl books. Douglas is characterised as 'Joshua': 'because he's the Prophet's helper and right-hand man, and carries out his orders. The Prophet thinks of things, and Joshua sees they're done.' Gadd appears as briefly as the 'Little Robin', due to her diminuitive stature and bright eyes, while Karpeles is shown only once as the Prophet's 'little secretary lady' and the 'little foot-page', since she flies off to run Sharp's errands.[22]

Madam and the Pixie appear in several books as maternal figures: they offer kindly advice and continue to critique the girls' dancing. For example, the Pixie's real caravan, 'The Fine Companion', is described in loving detail in *Queen of the Abbey Girls*, when Jen runs to the Pixie to ask her advice as to whether to or not to marry. But after major roles in the two books set at the vacation schools, the Pixie and Madam appear briefly in only two or three other books. Unlike characters from others of Oxenham's series, who wander in and out of each other's stories, they fall abruptly and completely out of the world of the Abbey Girls. It has been conjectured that Helen Kennedy North and D.C. Daking may have objected to their characterisation in the novels, and that there was a breach in Oxenham's personal friendship with them. It is also possible that Oxenham's move to Sussex in 1922 caused her to drop away from the London dance scene – and it must be remembered that she was a writer who drew much from life. Finally, it is also possible that as Oxenham wrote more of the romances of her Abbey Girls, she may have found it harder to sustain the characterisations of living people. As the Abbey Girls acquired babies, it also became harder to imagine them running off to dance schools for weeks at a time, and so the connection to the real world of dance was gradually toned down.

Certification and the vision of the folk dance

While Oxenham's and Sharp's visions of the higher purpose of folk dancing were not generally at odds, in one important area Oxenham obliquely criticised the Sharp empire: the 'certification' process. Amazingly, in these mass-market books for adolescent girls, Oxenham was quite specific and even scornful about those who attend just to improve their value as school teachers. As illustration of this, an older girl, known only as 'Advanced Certificate' or, sometimes, 'Miss Newcastle', comments that '... there are two kinds of students who come ; those who come from love of the dances and the 'folk' atmosphere; and those who want to learn and get certificates, just so that they can get better posts as teachers.'[23]

The relevance of this remark comes from the fact that one of Sharp's goals was to get English folk dancing on school curricula. To do this, he needed to standardise the dances, and to train teachers, through the means of graded classes and 'certificates'. The emphasis both in Oxenham's books as well as in real life on performing the dance in only one way no doubt sprang from this goal – these were classes, not social events, and participants were expected to tolerate considerable personal criticism in an effort to achieve the desired standard. For example, even Cicely and the other Abbey Girls are told bluntly by Madam after their first class at the Cheltenham summer school that: 'In knowledge of the dances you are quite up to this grade, but in style you are not. I've either got to put you down [a grade], or keep on [criticising] you till I get you right. I can't possibly pass mistakes such as you are making. You've been learning dances from the books, I suppose?'[24]

However, within the revival movement there were mixed feelings towards those teachers who wanted to 'get certificated' just so as to get better jobs rather than because they loved the dancing. Though one Abbey Girl observes that the former are just trying to better themselves, most of the girls are scornful of those who do not love the dancing as they do. Instead, Oxenham's clear and romantic feelings about the higher purpose of folk dancing is clearly expressed in several books by different characters, as in the following comments from 'Miss Newcastle':

> [I am only] a plain ordinary school teacher. I look after dozens of small children all day. But at night I teach folk-dancing and songs and drill to all kinds of girls – girls' clubs, Y.W.C.A. girls, unemployed girls, a big gym class on Mondays, and so on ... I'm keener on the big girls, and they simply live for their classes. They're in offices and shops,

or else they're little servant-girls from the country
with nowhere to go in the evenings, or typists and
cashiers; or girls still at school. I try to give them
with – no, through! – their folk-dance work a
wider outlook and an uplift which they seem to
feel the need of, and a touch of poetry and music
and art ... they respond most tremendously and
they do improve. *Those I've had for years are quite
different from the new-comers* [emphasis added].[25]

This view that folk dance can improve a working girl –
that it can make her less silly or flighty or can open her eyes to
the beauties that better educated and more sensitive people
see as a matter of course – is expressed frequently in the
Abbey Girls canon. For example, when Jen teaches folk
dances to the two groups of children, both the original village
inhabitants and the transient workers from 'Tin Town', she
finds:

> ... no difference at all in their delight in this new
> interest. The country dances made an instant
> appeal to both parties, and their enjoyment was
> obvious-pathetic, indeed, in its revelation of their
> need of some such outlet. They had felt it instinc-
> tively, but without understanding; had known
> they were dull, without knowing what to ask
> for ... [26]

Then Jen finds that the girls point their toes and hold up
their skirts, and that they are very self-conscious and silly; not
'natural' and 'relaxed' the way that Jen and her middle-class
friends had been at school. She complains to her father: 'they
work so frightfully hard! – far harder than they need. They
skip like horses, pulling their knees right up, for one thing.
They don't seem able to do it easily.' Her father suggests that
it is the responsibility of the teacher to set the right tone, to
help the girls get outside themselves and 'think bigger
things':

> There's education in it [folk dancing], in the sense
> of development; and character; and art. Give them
> all those, with our music and beautiful move-
> ments, and give them a common interest that will

hold them together and take them outside their
everyday lives; and you won't have done such a little thing, my dear.[27]

This concept of giving to those who need is expressed in
many of Oxenham's novels: whether through the medium of
the wealthy Joy taking East End crippled children out to the
country for a weekly drive or through the Abbey girls themselves teaching folk dance in the village in order to take poor
girls 'outside their everyday lives'. In *The New Abbey Girls*
(1923), for example, there is a lengthy sequence in which the
girls visit the Pixie's dance classes at a large Y.M.C.A. 'settlement house' in the slums. Pasty-faced and under-sized but
happy in their art, the boys love the dancing 'in the best way;
their dancing is as artistic, and as musical, and as full of
rhythm and beautiful movement, and of delight in it all, as
any you'd find anywhere, even at your Vacation Schools or big
town classes.'[28] While episodes of altruism like these help to
convince wealthy Joy how she should best use her money and
position to help others, Oxenham never challenged herself to
wonder if the dancing and the enhanced sense of artistry were
actually long-term solutions for poor, under-educated young
people sweating away in shops and factories; perhaps she
despaired of discovering the answer. But she clearly felt that
good, clean, wholesome entertainment, as opposed to that
found in music halls, jazz dancing, picture palaces or gin
shops, was at least a palliative.

Dances and dancing
Through Oxenham's detailed descriptions, we can observe
more about the kinds of dances done and the style in which
they were performed or taught and even the preferred costume during the early years of the English folk dance revival.
    For example, one characteristic about the dances from the
period of the 1910s and 20s captured by Oxenham was that
there appears to have been, ideally at least, little or no teaching at an evening dance. One went to classes in order to learn
the repertoire, oriented towards complex set dances, so that
one could go to dance parties. The programme was issued in
advance for a dance party, and participants came in evening
dress. By today's standards, the repertoire was limited. In one
essay on the topic of London dance parties, Oxenham noted

that Newcastle was a favourite: 'I have seen "Newcastle" danced four times through without a pause, then put in again later on as an extra, and danced three times more.' Other favourites are 'Hey Boys', 'Gathering Peascods', 'If All the World Were Paper' and 'The Old Mole'. Parties always included 'several' longways dances (Oxenham notes that 'The Butterfly', 'Christchurch Bells', 'Mary and Dorothy' and 'We Won't Go Home' were favourites with 'Haste to the Wedding' the most popular) and evenings usually ended with 'Sellenger's Round'.[29]

In the following quotation, however, we see that the rules about not teaching at parties could sometimes be relaxed. Here, the Pixie takes some of the Abbey Girls to a party in 'Dockland', a poor part of London. The Pixie acts as a lively M.C., making a point of mixing shy beginners with experienced dancers. In this session, they dance 'Rufty Tufty', 'Bonnets So Blue', 'Jenny Pluck Pears' and 'Mary and Dorothy'. The Pixie says:

> "It's a club members' party; just some jolly London girls and boys. We're all beginners; but we do know how to enjoy ourselves! The men wear these, over their shirts," and she showed coloured baldricks of red and green braid, to cross on the chest and back, and adorned with brilliant rosettes. "They like them; they feel dressed up. We don't have evening dress in Plaistow! The girls wear light frocks, if they have them; and most of them have. But they will wear these over their frocks, and then it doesn't really matter what's underneath," and she held up a tabard of bright blue, with a hole for the head, and bands of vivid braid to buckle under the arms, and rosettes at the waist-line to match those on the baldricks ... "we always used [these] in France, when we hauled in W.A.A.C.s or Y.M.C.A. ladies for partners ... Come along and find your partners! We shall do very easy dances to-night. I shall teach, you know; we still have to learn dances at our parties. There are always some who don't know them ..."[30]

That Oxenham as well as Sharp was particular about her dancing can be seen in the following excerpt from an early article on the topic of folk dancing that conveys the romanticism of Oxenham's writing and the flavour of the period as well as the degree of attention to detail that Sharp and his disciples demanded of this hobby:

> The other day I went to see some dancing, an ordinary school display, and now I see why [many people] say there is nothing in [country dancing] ... Those girls missed all the beautiful meaningful points of the dances. In "Gathering Peascods" they ran the rings, instead of slipping; they stood still after clapping, and the rhythmic continuous movement was ruined – you should see it done by those who know – and their clapping was anywhere, at waist level or shoulder high.
>
> Don't you know that you are doing when you run in and clap your hands? – how you are worshiping the holy tree on the village green, throwing up your arms to touch it and draw in the new life of spring to refresh and re-create your own body?
>
> The same movement, of course, that you get in "Sellenger" and in the introduction to "Mage," and "Newcastle."
>
> Those girls did not understand, or they could never have clapped in that slack, uninteresting, and ugly fashion.
>
> Then the lack of timing! Any number of steps was good enough for those girls to put to eight beats; eleven or fifteen pleased them quite well.
>
> In "Mary and Dorothy" they ran round in the rings in just as many steps as happened to be convenient, though eight definite beats are allowed; and they ran down the middle in five, or seven, or nine, just as many as they could squeeze into the two bars of music.
>
> Couldn't they hear the beat? Or had they never been told?
>
> But, worst of all, there was no sense of beauty in anything they did; it was all just a game. They took stately dances like "Hunsdon House" and "Oranges and Lemons," and raced through them at double speed, they left out "honours," messed

up their heys, cast off all over the place, turned
their backs on their partners in siding, and, of
course, their setting was dreadful; there were several distinct varieties, and one girl was most particular about pointing her toes.

Now those girls would not turn Beethoven's
music into a jig, or scribble over a beautiful picture, or scratch a statue, or sing oratorio music as
a comic song, or parody Browning; but they took
these three-hundred-year-old dances and romped
through them in any old way; caricatured them
without knowing it. They had not an atom of
respect for them.[31]

In the course of the Abbey Girls series, Oxenham frequently tells her girl readers the right way to perform certain
dances, as in the excerpt above. In *Jen of the Abbey School* she
also depicts for us a folk dance competition, in which the
heroines criticise the dancing skills as well as the attire of the
various teams (again drawing from life: Oxenham judged at
least a few dance competitions for the Girl Guides). We are
told that the most successful team costume is one in which
the girls dancing as girls wear one colour, and the girls dancing as men wear another; and, indeed, this standard, with the
colours of blue (men) and white (women) is the one Sharp
preferred. We are reminded that folk dancing in this period
was taken (or enforced) very seriously indeed.

Dancing attire appears frequently as an item of concern or
interest to Oxenham's characters, especially in the earlier
books. In the 1914 novel, *The Girls Of The Hamlet Club*, the
girls wear a costume described as that of a 'Puritan maiden': 'a
plain gray dress, with a broad white collar and cuffs and short
sleeves, and a little white hood'.[32] The costume, and especially the hood, is reminiscent of that worn by the seamstress
girls of Mary Neal's Esperance Society, leading one to believe
that Oxenham, ever a faithful recorder, saw performances of
this London-based group. Later, perhaps after Oxenham
went to Cheltenham herself and fell under Sharp's influence,
such finery was dismissed. As Sharp's war with Neal for control over the folk revival escalated, he came to regard the
Esperance girls' costume (and, indeed, the other romantic
trappings and aspects of the 'Merrie Olde Englande' movement) as vulgar, and stressed that true country dancing

required no special costume or preparation (though his people were still dancing in evening dress). He lectured that:

> ... any spectacular qualities that the Country
> Dance may possess are fortuitous, or, rather, the
> inevitable outcome of the perfect fashioning of
> means to end. Its beauty, being implicit, needs,
> therefore, no artificial embellishment. An elabo-
> rate theatrical setting would be as irrelevant and
> impertinent as for the dancers to deck themselves
> in rich and fanciful costumes.[33]

Under his spell, the obedient Oxenham then reworks her
characters' costume, so that, by 1920, Cicely is described as
wearing 'a cotton frock of dull Liberty red, plain in the
bodice, short and full in the skirt, short sleeved and cut low at
the neck, with wide white collar and cuffs, and a ribbon of the
same rich red tucked into her dark curly hair'. Neophyte Joy
wonders if everyone dresses up. Cicely answers: 'We all dress
alike, in any colour we choose, but all with dresses like this,
and those!' and she thrust out her foot, in a white stocking
and low black slipper with cross-bands of black elastic. 'All
the white feet look rather jolly ...'[34] As the series progresses,
the typical Abbey Girl dance dress is standardised as a simple
frock (often with material handwoven by the Pixie) with a full
skirt and a fitted bodice and short sleeves; attire that con-
trasts with the tubular shape and bobbed hair of the giddy
flapper more representative of the period.

Oxenham also echoes Sharp's emphasis on 'gay simplicity', with regard to the unostentatious presentation, and even
the nature, of English folk dance. The Abbey girls continually remind each other that they are not performing dances in
order to show off; they are simply enjoying them. Socialising
and talking while dancing is not merely permitted; it is
encouraged. When little Jen is nervous about dancing with
the important May Queens, Joan admonishes her: 'Don't
think about yourself, that's all; there's no time for that in this
kind of dancing!'[35] In evocative phrases, Oxenham restates
Sharp's dicta, as here, when the girls dance Rufty Tufty in the
Abbey's cloister garth:

> The movements of the dance, the running steps,
> the leading out and back in couples, were as sim-

ple and natural as the little tune, and all seemed
strangely in keeping with the sheer simplicity of
the buildings around the garth, the strong pure
lines of the Early English windows, the arches of
the chapter-house, the wide, dignified refectory.
Nowhere was there any ornament, any unnecessary decoration; that had been forbidden by the
severe Cistercian rule under which the Abbey had
been built. The music had no note that could have
been spared, the dance no unnecessary movement; no fancy or decorative attitude was even
hinted at.[36]

Conclusion

All ninety of Oxenham's novels contain a consistent moral
and aesthetic ethos composed of the love of nature and of
God, of adherence to honour and duty, of loyalty and fairness.
Her forty-volume Abbey Girls series expresses these attributes in part through the characters' shared enjoyment of folk
music and dance. Oxenham herself loved music and dance
and wrote about both expressively and with passion. For
those who enjoy romantic novels from the early part of the
century, Oxenham's books are still engaging and accessible.

The earliest Abbey Girl books also represent an easy way
for the reader of today to capture the sense of excitement and
romance that participants in the early folk revival experienced. Under Sharp's inspiration, those dancers from the
early years felt that they were saving dances and songs that
were about to be swept away by popular, urban culture. They
dreamed of giving these uniquely English gifts back to the
people, making England a better place. Cecil Sharp may have
had his faults, but one of his most shining virtues was his
ability to inspire and excite others about folk music and
dance. In reading Oxenham's works, we too can fall under his
spell.

That Oxenham's writings promoted the Sharp philosophy
is clear; it is also apparent that that one reason for Sharp's
own success in controlling and expanding the English Folk
Dance Society was that he tapped into the general sensibilities of the Edwardian period and the artistic and philan-
thropic aspirations that Oxenham was herself a part of and

portrayed so clearly. For all of these reasons, Elsie J. Oxenham's view of the folk revival is an important one.

Notes

1. 'Douglas Kennedy states that over the years he has been struck by the number of people who have told him that they were first attracted to the folk movement [by reading Oxenham's works]' from 'Elsie J. Oxenham; Chronicler of the Folk Movement,' by Joan Peck, *English Dance & Song*. 43, No.2, June 1981.

2. This theory is argued persuasively by Hilary Clare in the May 2000 issue of *The Abbey Chronicle* (No. 35, 36–43).

3. Information on Elsie Jeanette Oxenham's life comes from Monica Godfrey's *Elsie Jeanette Oxenham And Her Books*, (London: Autolycus Publications, 1979).

4. Space precludes discussion here of Oxenham's charming and distinctive May Queen ceremony and imagery which appears to have been based on the similar ceremony invented by John Ruskin for the Whitelands Teachers' Training College, in Chelsea. Oxenham may have seen a ceremony at first hand, or her friend and idol, Helen Kennedy North, who had been a physical instruction educator at Whitelands, may have shared her experiences with her friend.

5. Oxenham, *The New Abbey Girls*, (London: Collins, 1923), p. 132.

6. Though written and published in 1927, this is one of the many 'retrospective' novels, which takes place during and immediately after the events of *The Abbey Girls Go Back to School*, believed to have been written in 1919 or 1920. Thus, the Director is referred to as still living (Sharp died in 1924), but, on the other hand, the detailed description of the folk dance competition in this novel probably comes from Oxenham's own experience in the later 1920s, after she had moved from London.

7. Oxenham, *Jen of the Abbey School*, (London: Collins, 1949 (1927)), 34–36.

8. Boyes, Georgina, *The Imagined Village; Culture, Ideology and the English Folk Revival*, (Manchester and New York: Manchester University Press, 1993), p. 95.

9. *Ibid.*, p. 99.

10. Oxenham, *The Abbey Girls Go Back To School*, (London: Collins, 1922), p. 172.

11. Oxenham, *Queen Of The Abbey Girls*, (London: Collins, 1947 (1926)), p. 187

12. Oxenham was not the only writer to refer to Sharp as 'The Director': popular and prolific novelist E.V. Lucas (brother of Perceval, a member of Sharp's original morris demonstration team) also described him as such in his 1912 work, *London Lavender*.

13. Oxenham, *The Abbey Girls In Town*, (London: Collins, 1925), 74–78.

14. Oxenham, *The Abbey Girls Go Back To School*, p. 221.

15. *Ibid.*, p. 260.

16. *Ibid.*, pp. 202–203.

17. The Camp Fire movement was founded by American educator Luther Halsey Gulick in Maine in 1910. A more artistic and romantic organisation than the drill-oriented Girl Guides, girls assumed Native American names, wore fringed brown Indian dresses and moccasins, and focused on crafts and camping activities.

18. Oxenham, *Two Joans At The Abbey*, (London: Collins, 1945), pp. 40–41.

19. Oxenham, *The Abbey Girls Go Back To School*, p. 197. It should be noted, however, that Oxenham's characters know full well that Madam only offers such criticism to those persons who are keen enough to want to improve and

tough enough to not mind it.

20. *Ibid.*, p. 193.
21. Oxenham, 'Folk Dancing,' *Every Girl's Annual*, 1923, p. 44.
22. Oxenham, *The Abbey Girls Go Back To School*, pp. 175, 301 and 174.
23. *Ibid.*, p. 133. Miss Newcastle has been identified as Catherine Ord, head of folk dancing at that time in Newcastle.
24. *Ibid.*, p. 116.
25. *Ibid.*, pp. 154–155.
26. Oxenham, *The Abbey Girls Go Back To School*, p. 54
27. *Ibid.*, pp. 57–60.
28. Oxenham, *The New Abbey Girls*, p. 200.
29. Oxenham, 'Folk Dancing,' *Every Girl's Annual*, 1923, p. 35.
30. Oxenham, *The Abbey Girls In Town*, p. 267.
31. Oxenham, 'Folk Dancing,' pp. 36–37.
32. Oxenham, *The Girls Of The Hamlet Club*, (London: Chambers, 1914), p. 221.
33. Sharp, Cecil, *The Country Dance Book, Volume II*, (London: Novello & Co., Ltd., 3rd ed., 1927), p. 62.
34. Oxenham, *The Abbey Girls*, (London: Collins, 1920), p. 85.
35. *Ibid.*, p. 262.
36. Oxenham, *Queen of the Abbey Girls*, p. 26.

Maud Karpeles and George Bernard Shaw. *Credit: EFDSS*

'The lady that is with you ...': Maud Pauline Karpeles (1885–1976) and the Folk Revival

Georgina Boyes

Maud Karpeles' involvement in the Folk Revival can be concisely summarised. She was, her most perceptive obituarist concluded, 'impelled ... to project into futurity the dogma and interpretations of Cecil Sharp.'[1] Her devotion to the material, institutional and theoretical legacy of Cecil James Sharp (1859–1924), England's foremost collector of folksong and dance, was the defining cause of her life. But it proved to be an equivocal choice. Her passionate commitment to the man and his ideas took her into a career that contained achievement and vilification in almost equal measure. Association with the Folk Revival which Sharp created provided opportunities to employ her intellectual and organisational abilities at national and international level – in spheres that the daughter of wealthy Victorian parents might otherwise never have considered, let alone accessed. But, sharing some of his character traits and championing his approach to folk art, Karpeles became a convenient surrogate to those unwilling to make a direct personal attack on such a revered figure as Sharp himself. Her close association with him also provided justification for her own subsequent work to be undervalued or ignored – allowing her to be dismissed as a mere continuation, rather than considered as a researcher and administrator in her own right.

Tellingly, although Sharp died in 1924 and Karpeles continued a high profile involvement in Folklore Studies until
her death in 1976, her autobiography was not accepted for
publication on the grounds that it did not contain enough
new information about the work of Cecil Sharp to warrant
printing.[2] And even today – during a period of extensive academic reassessment of the Folk Revival – Karpeles' role and
significance remain almost entirely unexamined.

This continued absence of analysis is difficult to justify. As
a leading figure in the English Folk Revival for sixty-seven
years, editor and writer of a substantial body of works on folk-
song, dance and custom, initiator and chief administrator of
the International Folk Music Council, Karpeles exerted considerable influence on the practice and theory of Folk Studies
for much of the twentieth century. As a collector of songs and
dances in Britain, Continental Europe and North America,
her work was unusually wide-ranging and undertaken during
a period when English collecting was mostly dormant. She
was equally prominent in applied Folklore. Sharp's regular
dancing partner for illustrated lectures, Karpeles was a key
member of the English Folk Dance Society's demonstration
team and a teacher, examiner and competition adjudicator at
its highest level. As a practitioner and authority, her views on
the performance of English historical and traditional dances
were crucial to the development of repertoire and style in the
growing revival movement. Well connected, independently
wealthy and motivated by unquestioning enthusiasm,
Karpeles was also the archetypal admirer that Sharp fostered
in his early campaign to make folksongs and dances acceptable to the Establishment. In a field which has scant documentation of the attitudes of the individuals involved –
particularly those of women who formed the majority of the
Folk Revival's supporters – her extended personal accounts
are invaluable. But rather than providing a source for funda-
mental research, Karpeles and her many-faceted career are
virtually invisible.

Why is this? Aside from Cecil Sharp, Karpeles is probably
the most familiar name associated with the early days of the
English Folk Dance Society[3] – but her name is virtually the
only fact known about her. For most dancers, singers and
researchers working in the Folk Revival, Maud Karpeles

exists as a concept rather than an individual. She is 'Miss Karpeles', the original purist, leader of a generation of reactionary and repressed folk dancing spinsters. Persistent reference to her by a maiden title goes far beyond conventional forms of address. Our idea of 'Miss Karpeles' draws purposefully on cultural stereotypes of narrow-minded old maids and hectoring schoolmistresses. Her name is a powerful signifier – to hear it is to have full access to perceptions of her character, lifestyle and ideology.

Within the Folk Dance Revival, however, such stereotypes have additional dimensions. From 1904, Sharp had encouraged women's performance of morris and sword dances which he had originally collected from men, proposing that, in the new circumstances of the Revival, this did 'no great violence' to tradition. Subsequently, his successful campaign to ensure folksong and dance were required elements of the national curriculum drew large numbers of women schoolteachers into the English Folk Dance Society. From his death, however, as Allison Thompson's paper highlights, these women were increasingly criticised for joining simply 'to improve their professional prospects' – a situation tolerated only for its substantial contribution of membership and examination fees to Society coffers. At the same time, voices began to be raised against women's performance of 'male' traditional dances. By the early 1930s, official publications of the English Folk Dance and Song Society increasingly represented many women's general participation as a disadvantage:

> In the successful rural centres there is the balanced proportion of men and women dancers which is essential to the permanent re-establishment of the country dance in every day life ... In the cities and towns the position is far less encouraging and this year in particular [1933–34] has proved a period of exceptional difficulty. There exists in the towns a very large number of enthusiastic and experienced dancers, there persists a demand for personal instruction, especially among women; but what is conspicuous by its absence is the social group of men and women meeting together to dance for recreation ... The stronghold of the E.F.D.S. in the majority of towns remains the dusty, draughty drill hall with its

questionable piano and it complete absence of
warmth, gaiety and decoration, where some twenty or thirty women in every-day dress await the
arrival of the visiting teacher.[4]

Douglas Kennedy (1893–1988), Director of the English
Folk Dance and Song Society from 1925 to 1961, also used the
Society's magazine to propose that the majority of the general public were prejudiced against folk dancing because 'its
practice was linked in the minds of many with the crank or
with women and children.'[5] 'The bulk of our active members
are women,' he wrote in an article on recruitment in 1946, but
the main object of the Society was 'the active enrolment of a
Member or an Associate' which he defined as 'rendering
down an ordinary chap into a dancer'. Women could, therefore, most helpfully increase membership, 'by concealing
their present disproportion behind the curtain of the 'private'
type of event while we continue to encourage the growth of
men's Morris and Sword and mixed teams of Country dancers
so that the Society can more frequently appear in public and
do more recruiting.'[6] And although they paid full membership fees, Kennedy later took this informal position further,
ruling that women members of the English Folk Dance and
Song Society would not obtain tickets for summer schools
and festival events unless they could produce a male partner
to accompany them. Meanwhile at Cecil Sharp House, the
headquarters of the English Folk Dance and Song Society, he
noted with satisfaction, 'a rather large army of unpartnered
girls' had been driven away from weekly square dances.
    But if women in general were represented as a problem for
the English Folk Dance and Song Society, responsibility for a
situation in which 'unfortunately males were in the minority'
and a host of other failings within the organisation was
specifically tied to the influence of one woman. Karpeles was
an outspoken proponent of women's right to perform sword
and morris dances as part of the Revival, so 'Maud's hand on
the helm', leading figures insisted, was the cause of the
'unbalanced growth' in which 'the greater part of support
came from the women', the inter-war 'influx of teachers' and
the 'reason the Society soon found itself in a rut' after Sharp's
death.[7] Such conclusions overlook the demographic effects of
the First World War, but more importantly they comprehen-
sively ignore the history of a movement which had seen many

of its greatest successes with women dancers, administrators and schoolteachers making up a great proportion of its membership and Maud Karpeles in a leading role. They are, however, still widely accepted.

Decades of general and specific scapegoating have proved remarkably effective in minimising the significance and denigrating the nature of Karpeles' activities. Where her work is discussed, it is now usually prefixed or sometimes solely represented by the information that she was Cecil Sharp's 'amanuensis' – the choice of word and its habitual application to her reinforcing her image as an archaic adjunct rather than a capable individual. And sadly, her parents' choice of first name for their daughter inadvertently contributes to a caricature which misrepresents her character and scholarship. As the summation of all that is least admired in the Revival, 'Miss Karpeles' is fully institutionalised – the process of its continued reproduction as manifest in Peter Kennedy's 1998 article 'Everybody's Folk' in the members' magazine of the English Folk Dance and Song Society,[8] as in the conversational 'Poor you' which invariably greeted the news that I was researching her for this paper.

As a result, Maud Karpeles' extraordinary contributions to the Folk Revival have been ignored or distorted. English field collectors of her generation – and later – offer little that can be compared with the range and depth of her experience. Initially, in 1911 and 1912 she simply accepted Sharp's invitation to join him at customary performances like the Whitsun morris dance at Bampton in Oxfordshire, the Hobby Horse ceremonies at Minehead in Somerset and Padstow in Cornwall and the Helston Furry Dance in Cornwall – where she had her first taste of participant observation:

> Not being in our best clothes – as is demanded by tradition – we had to tag on at the end of the long procession, but we enjoyed ourselves none the less for that.[9]

Later expeditions, however, proved rather more challenging:

> The finest of all the Sword Dances comes from Handsworth, a suburb of Sheffield. As with many

of the Sword Dance teams the dancers are miners; 'artists every one of them' was Cecil Sharp's pronouncement on those from whom he noted the dance. This was no exaggeration. I had the good fortune to accompany Cecil to Sheffield on Easter Monday of 1913 when the dancers were performing in a parade for the benefit of the local hospital. They had arranged to give a special performance for us and a few friends and we repaired to a sordid public-house in a mean street in which a noisy crowd was disporting itself. It seemed to be an unlikely setting for a display of artistry, but as soon as the dance started one was caught up in its rhythm and the material world around ceased to exist.[10]

And by the time she had worked with Sharp on the extended lecture and field trips in America during 1916 and 1917–18, Karpeles had become the most experienced of the new generation of English collectors. Sharp's description of their timetable and conditions at the start of their journey giving some idea of what this new work entailed:

Maud and I left New York in tropical heat on Sunday afternoon, got to Knoxville on Monday at 1.30, left for Copper Hill an hour or so later, arriving at this very primitive little mining village at 10 P.M. Our train left at 6.30 A.M. yesterday (Tuesday), got on to Murphy at 11, where we changed onto the Southern Railway, and eventually arrived here at 11.30 P.M. – or, rather, what was left of us. Maud's suit case was lost – I am almost afraid, stolen – between Knoxville and Copper Hill, which made the journey very uncomfortable for her. But, despite the heat, the dust, the lack of food, the swarms of flies, hay fever, asthma, etc., it was a wonderful trip.[11]

Within a few months, Karpeles was working independently, participating in and contextualising sometimes controversial performances:

At Hyden we were fortunate enough to see undis-

turbed a good set of dancers and, a few days later,
after Cecil Sharp had been taken ill, I went to a
'bean-stringing' in the neighbourhood, where I
witnessed and took part in the dance. It was performed in a small, unventilated room about
twelve feet square into which thirty or forty people besides the dancers managed to squeeze themselves. Set-running has a bad name in the
mountains, possibly because of Puritan prejudices, but more probably because it leads often to
drinking and shooting.[12]

These comments on the background to her joining in and
recording set-running are typically brief and understated, but
they offer a marked contrast to the work of her contemporaries. In England, collection might still include an invitation
for a singer or dancers to come to the house of a local notable
to perform on the collector's terms or, more demandingly,
involve notation in a working class home or pub. Even in the
cause of rescuing an imperilled national heritage, English
revivalists did not normally go off alone and volunteer themselves as partners in boozy dances – particularly those which
might end in exchanges of gunfire.

Karpeles' approach to collection – particularly travelling,
living and recording in remote, alien cultures – has few direct
parallels in English Folklore Studies. She made her first
extended solo field trips in Newfoundland in 1929 and 1930.
At this time, the only practical means of travel to the isolated
'outport' coastal settlements of this North Atlantic island was
by open boat. Triumphing over consistent seasickness and
dirt roads, she collected 191 versions of 91 songs. 'There is
singing and dancing wherever she goes' recorded one
charmed performer; she was 'like some one you have known
very well who has gone away and then come back', confirmed
another. 'I felt that remark was a genuine endorsement', she
told a Folk-Lore Society meeting the following year.[13] In contrast to many later folklorists, she also made a practice of
revisiting singers and dancers in areas where she had worked
– including return trips to Appalachia in 1950 and in 1970, at
the age of 84, to Newfoundland. Here, she was again involved
in recording some of the singers who had originally performed for her – and their children.

An approachable and open-minded collector, Karpeles

Maud Karpeles dancing. *Credit: EFDSS*

was happy to adapt to new media and engage with all kinds of traditions and performers. She was more than usually alive to the significance of contexts of performance and accompanied her dance notations with pen-portraits of the communities and individuals involved – even including local sayings associated with the performers' appearance for the morris dances she collected at Upton-on-Severn and an outline of the role of the Abram Urban District Council's use of concrete posts in attempts to retain a traditional dance site 'for the people of Abram'. Working with Cecil Sharp's daughter, Susannah, during 1928 she collected the Royton Morris, it was the beginning of a wider association with previously under-appreciated north-western dance traditions. The Royton dancers were, she recalled, 'an extraordinarily friendly group' and she saw their performance as the 'most important' she had ever found.

Evidence of her success as a fieldworker at this time can be gauged from her thoughtful handling of the 1929 collection of the Britannia Coco-Nut Dances detailed in Theresa Buckland's article as well as from the English Folk Dance Society annual report for 1930–31, where there are references to an article on square dance figures she had collected from New York State and a book of twelve country dances collected from Northumberland, Cumberland, Devonshire, Vermont in the United States and Newfoundland. The following year then saw her detailed article on the form and context of the Abram Circle Dance.[14] Karpeles also continued to collect folksongs, shanties and carols in England through the 1920s and 30s – and unlike Cecil Sharp, she positively encouraged others to go out and discover folksongs and dances for themselves.[15] She organised Phil Tanner's earliest recording session for Columbia in 1937 – he was, she said, 'one of the best singers I have ever heard', and in 1946, was responsible for the English Folk Dance and Song Society's first recordings of 'authentic folk music performed by traditional instrumentalists', which featured ceremonial dance tunes played by William Kimber and George Tremain. Her ears always open for a traditional tune, she even invited an old sailor she heard singing in the street back to her flat to notate his shanties and then arranged for him to perform at Cecil Sharp House.

It is characteristic of her research methods and approach that her views on the inter-relationship between performance and context were far in advance of her time – embracing participant research and a role for the Revival. In 1931, she proposed that 'the folk dancer cannot appreciate his dances to the full unless he has some knowledge of the conditions and events which have influenced and prompted their growth; and the folklorist cannot afford on his side to ignore the living matter which is presented him by the folk dancer.' Even the august membership of the Folk-Lore Society were encouraged with gentle humour to reach a better understanding of the genre by taking part. It was never, she suggested, too late to start dancing:

> The happiest and most satisfactory state of affairs is, of course, that in which the folk dancer and the folklorist are combined in one and the same person. Some of our folk dancers are endeavouring to become folklorists in a mild way ... Is it too much to ask that you in your turn should avail yourselves of the opportunities afforded by The English Folk Dance Society and become folk dancers? And lest anyone should hesitate to do so out of respect to the dignity of his years, I would tell him or her that it has been proved beyond all doubt that the most suitable age to start dancing is the age you happen to be.[16]

Without the intelligence and administrative drive provided by Maud Karpeles, it is possible that the Folk Revival would barely have survived Sharp's death. Her commitment to seeing Sharp's work continue was absolute. His will appointed her as his literary executor, responsible for all aspects of the publication of his extensive English and American collection of dances and songs. She ably fulfilled this role whilst acting as Honorary Secretary of the English Folk Dance Society – its activities and membership expanding whilst under her influence. With Douglas Kennedy (organising director) and Ralph Vaughan Williams (musical adviser), she also made up the Society's board of artistic control. No aspect of Sharp's practical and theoretical legacy of Folk Revival were untouched by her influence. After her death, Douglas Kennedy, who had been amongst her most vocal opponents, reflected that:

> When Cecil Sharp fell ill and died in 1924 his
> mantle had already fallen upon Maud. She at once
> took over responsibility for the literary output
> and completed such publications as were in the
> pipe line. During the coming years she continued
> to sift through the collected material, both dance
> and song, producing books in the form that the
> changing needs required. Sharp's personal friends
> who had feared a complete shut down when the
> great man died were filled with admiration at
> Maud's resourceful ability.[17]

She was however, far more than a capable administrator,
dancer and researcher of traditions. In stark opposition to the
narrow stereotype of 'Miss Karpeles' which travesties her life
and character, Maud Pauline Karpeles was a woman of liberal
sympathies and cosmopolitan background. She was born in
London on the 12 November 1885, third child of J.N.
Karpeles and Emily A. Raphael (1861–1914) in a family of
four sisters and one brother.[18] The Karpeles were affluent but
– as her unpublished autobiography makes clear – their
'almost luxurious' life was not so much due to her father's
acumen as a tea merchant as to her mother's inheritance from
her family, who were bankers. And perhaps the lack of
warmth which she says characterised the family's relationships, was a reflection of this marital disappointment, as well
as her mother's chronic ill heath. It was a rather sombre early
childhood.

Karpeles' education was limited in scope and, to her
regret, far from academic. She was taught by a governess at
home and then attended Kensington High School. At the age
of fifteen she was sent as a boarder to Hamilton House in
Tunbridge Wells where she was very happy and, she thought,
the only girl who spent her holidays at home looking forward
to going back to school. To her great satisfaction, she eventually became head girl at Hamilton House. But despite the
ability clearly attested by her later work, she did not go on to
University; girls in her circle were, she recalled, not encouraged to show intellectual tendencies.

Branches of Karpeles' family were active in political and
artistic affairs in England and on the Continent. Although he
had taken British citizenship before her birth, her father was
born in Hamburg and many of her relations still lived in

Germany. After leaving school, Karpeles spent some months in Berlin with her father's sister, Gonni, who was a painter. Gonni was married to Julius Stern, the Director of the National Bank and at their house Karpeles met many of the leading cultural figures of the day, among them the theatre director, Gordon Craig and Isadora Duncan, the proponent of Greek dance. She also records being charmed by the lively personality of the composer Ferraccio Busoni. Returning to London around 1906, she became involved in politics through the influence of her mother's brother, Sir Herbert Raphael, Liberal Member of Parliament for South Derbyshire and a Trustee of the National Portrait Gallery.[19] Raphael and his wife Rosalie Costar were childless and the young Karpeles was often invited to stay with them at Allestree Hall in Derby. Here she met many politicians and developed an interest in current affairs which took her into membership of the Fabian Society – there were numerous heated and enjoyable debates between H.G. Wells and George Bernard Shaw which Wells usually lost, she recalled. She also attended meetings in support of that longstanding cultural cause, the movement to establish a National Theatre.

More fundamentally, her increasing political awareness led her to practical involvement in social work. A talk at school about Dr Barnardo's campaigns for homeless children had already heightened her perception of the gap between her own privileged circumstances and the poverty that existed all around her. Now in her early twenties, she volunteered to work at the Mansfield House Settlement in Canning Town in London. Founded in the 1880s as 'experiments in religious and social action',[20] by the early years of the twentieth century, settlements had diversified and were to be found in most cities. Karpeles records that she saw her involvement with the movement as the chance to be of use – and certainly spending three or four days a week with the Invalid Children's Aid Association visiting houses and hospitals in East Ham and Barking can hardly have been a glamourous option.

Settlements also had a recreational side. Each week, with her younger sister Helen (1887–1976), Karpeles ran a meeting of the Guild of Play for children at Mansfield House. Teaching action songs and maypole dances was, she records, a real delight. And it was in search of new material for these meetings that in May 1909, she and Helen went 'out of curiosity' to a Festival of Folk Song and Dance which formed part of the Shakespeare Festival at Stratford-on-Avon. Karpeles had always been deeply moved by music and the traditional dance tunes entranced her:

> ... we stayed the whole day, spellbound by what we saw and more particularly in what we heard. The dancing was crude, but the music, the like of which we had not heard before, enchanted us.[21]

In September 1909, when Cecil Sharp, who had been one of the judges at Stratford, opened his own School of Morris Dancing at the Chelsea Physical Training College in London, Maud and Helen immediately joined.

Karpeles and others have published numerous accounts of the events which flowed from these encounters.[22] Maud and her sister seized whatever opportunity arose to take part in this new and exciting activity. They supplemented their Chelsea classes with other opportunities to learn, formed their friends into a Folk-Dance Club, took examinations and trained other dancers, gave charity performances and travelled the country providing illustrations for Sharp's lectures on folk dance. Their early commitment was rewarded on the 6 December 1911, when Sharp invited members of their Folk-Dance Club to provide the nucleus of his new Revival organisation, the English Folk-Dance Society – with Maud taking a place on the committee and Helen acting as its honorary secretary.

The new Society grew rapidly and fuelled by Sharp's insistence on an examination-based approach to revival soon created a considerable burden of administration. Initially, this was almost entirely undertaken by Sharp himself, but in 1913 he developed neuritis of the arm and was for a time unable to write. Aged 27, Maud Karpeles volunteered to help. Her own description of this is brief and understated:

> I offered my services as an amanuensis and from that time until his death in 1924 I was closely associated with his work. At first I used to pay daily visits to Uxbridge from London and afterwards I lived for the most part with the family.[23]

The consequences of her increasing involvement were,

however, far-reaching. Personally, her 'close association' with Sharp has provoked continuing innuendo in the Folk Revival, paradoxically side by side with her portrayal as archetypal spinster. During his lifetime, within the English Folk Dance Society, Karpeles was 'sometimes irreverently known as 'Mrs. Sharp'[24] and her unpublished autobiography is unequivocal about her feelings for him. Rather than a fifty-odd musician, of uncertain health and temper, prone to gout, asthma and controversy, she tells us that early in their rela-tionship she saw him as a knight in shining armour. Her descriptions of cooking for him and sharing meals in their New York hotel on visits to America are tender miniatures of a home life that might have been. She nursed him when he was ill during their Appalachian trips, sleeping in his room with the approval, she said, of his semi-invalid wife. In her 80s, asked by a BBC interviewer what the great collector Cecil Sharp was like, her immediate response was as considered and definite as it is unexpected: 'He was handsome,' she said. When Sharp died, Karpeles went away alone and experienced something close to a nervous breakdown. She said in her autobiography that she loved him – and there seems little doubt that she did. Whether the emotion was given any fur-ther physical expression than a dance partnership is, I think, of essential concern only to her, Cecil and Constance Sharp. But the speculation which surrounds the relationship is an unacknowledged element in the dismissive attitudes to her work found later in the English Folk Revival.

After Sharp's death, Karpeles devoted herself to ensuring that his ideas and the organisation he devised to embody them lived on, particularly through her editions of his collec-tions and work with the International Folk Music Council. But though widely regarded as 'a mainstay of the EFDSS for many years',[25] her role as a senior administrator in the Society Sharp created was, in fact, greatly curtailed. Her sister Helen [Karpeles] Kennedy and brother-in-law, Douglas Kennedy enjoyed long, active careers leading the English Folk Dance and Song Society and after their retirement were made vice-presidents. But following a bitter dispute over the exercise of Sharp's copyright, which she oversaw as his literary executor, Karpeles was left with little option in 1936 but to tender her resignation from its National Executive. Accepting the offer of a seat on the Society's Board of Examiners, she was subse-

quently informed by Douglas Kennedy that taking this position debarred her from all dance teaching. By 1938, she held
only a place on the Library Committee and an ordinary membership in the Society of which she was a founder member.
Omitting any reference to disputes over copyright, later
Revival sources cite her inflexible adherence to Sharp's views
on the use of examinations and promotion of folk dancing
through schools as the causes of her unsuitability.

There is, however, a still more unpleasant background to
her exclusion. Her systematic removal from positions within
the English Folk Dance and Song Society began in the early
1930s, coinciding with the increased criticism of women's
participation in the movement. The most outspoken opponent of women's activities and prominence in the hierarchy of
the Folk Revival was Rolf Gardiner (1902–71), a founder
member of the Travelling Morrice, chief theoretician and
moving spirit behind the exclusively male Morris Ring. 'I
still hold to my unaltered opinion,' he wrote in *English Dance
& Song* in 1936 'that the leaders of our revival should have
had the moral courage to forbid women's Morris; it was a bad
lapse in taste and wisdom that ever permitted such a contra-
diction in terms.'[26] He repeatedly complained of a situation in
which 'women flocked to the schools and dominated the
Society's branches'. 'Men were in a hopeless minority,' he
wrote. 'It was a most unnatural state of affairs.'[27] The means
by which the emergence of the Morris Ring and revised attitudes to social dance were dynamics in the marginalisation of
women in the movement has been outlined elsewhere,[28] but in
the case of Karpeles herself there is a further element of opposition which has not hitherto been explored. Karpeles parents
did not practice any religion and her upbringing was almost
entirely secular. Her parents' families were, however, Jewish,
and the Karpeles, originally from Eastern Europe, now mainly lived in Germany.

Gardiner, an early and consistent advocate of Fascism,
held strong opinions on the subject of Jews. Shortly after a
day long celebration of his marriage at the headquarters of
the English Folk Dance and Song Society in 1932, he provided his reactions to Hitler's new National Socialist government for a book published in Germany. 'The Jews who had
come from Russia, Poland and other Slav countries to
Germany during and after the [First] War,' he wrote, 'had

added a very unpleasant element to German Jewry.' They were, he averred, 'restless Ahasueruses' who when they first arrived in Berlin and Vienna brought 'the smell of Asia with them in their beards.'[29]

Recent apologists have claimed that Gardiner only 'flirted with Fascism' and that he 'backed off when Hitler's agenda became apparent',[30] or that embracing a different form of Fascism to that proposed by Oswald Mosley's British Union of Fascists somehow made his ideology less genuine. Alternatively, it is suggested, even if he was a Fascist, his actions and ideas were never of significant influence within the Folk Revival. None of these proposals is borne out by contemporary evidence. 'Every nation today,' Gardiner wrote in 1932, 'requires a form of Fascism to rescue it from the pitfalls of its own self-sufficiency.' He travelled regularly and extensively in Germany during the 1920s and 30s, returning to lecture appreciatively on a range of German initiatives from rural housing and work camps to farming and folk dance. In 1938, praising the results of the Nazi government's policies – it had already introduced the Nuremberg Laws, which removed most Jews' civil rights and barred them from employment, opened concentration camps and imprisoned critics like Pastor Niemöller without trial – he proposed that:

> In Germany the opportunities for cultivating local values have increased rather than decreased as the result of intenser national union. Although the nation is powerfully self-conscious of its wholeness, the roots of this feeling are deep in the soil of infinite local variety. This is of course one of the many truths obscured by our liar-press.

And even as late as 1943, put on record that he saw Nazism merely as 'fanatical impatience'.[31]

Gardiner, who was partly of Austrian descent and had studied German at Cambridge, dismissed most British forms of Fascist ideology as too 'suburban'. Instead, he preferred to draw on the combination of misogyny, racism and rule by secret male societies embraced by the German Freikorps, many of whose members went on to provide significant proportions of the SS. As Stephen Corrsin's paper makes clear, there were direct theoretical and personal links between Gardiner   and   several   high-ranking   activists   in   the

Nazification of scholarship. But it was the work of Richard
Wolfram (1901–95), which had the deepest influence on
Gardiner and through him to ideas within the English Folk
Revival. Wolfram gave papers at English Folk Dance and
Song Society meetings, attended the Society's 1935
International Folk Dance Conference, published articles and
– from December 1946 – contributed reports on how research
had fared in Austria 'in spite of the difficulties of the war' to
the Society's *Journal*. He was also a leading provider of theo-
ries of 'intellectual inheritance' to the SS and associated with
the deportation of anti-Nazi Norwegian students to concentration camps.[32]

Describing the first part of Wolfram's monograph on the
sword dance, *Schwerttanz und Männerbünde* (*Sword Dancing
and Male Groups*), as a 'great book', Gardiner quoted from it
approvingly in *English Dance and Song*. He then used English
Folk Dance and Song Society publications and Morris Ring
meetings to disseminate his own extension of Wolfram's the-
ories of sword dance as the ritual of secret male societies to
morris dance. His proposals continue to re-echo unwittingly
through some parts of the Folk Dance movement today:

> Now that at last the Morris Ring is beginning to
> rescue the Morris from the movement, permit an
> ancient among heretics to speak again. The time
> which regarded the Morris as 'healthy exercise,' as
> a worthy alternative to ping-pong, tennis or golf,
> is passing; soon the sight of concave-chested,
> bespectacled suburbans prancing over the school-
> room floor in rubber-soled (insulating) shoes will
> become rarer ... And the Morris will become itself
> again, the dance of men, sworn to manhood, fiery
> ecstasy, ale, magic and fertility ... It will become
> the communion rite of clubs and 'secret societies,'
> of lazy rascals, roisterers and scallywags, of
> princes among these ... the men's dance will
> return to the men, an ever-new, evolving, fertile
> tradition.[33]

Gardiner's consistently expressed views and specific associations cannot be sanitised in hindsight, excused on their historical context, or ignored. A feudal Fascist aiming to exert
'power in the lanes and hamlets of England', critical of phys-

ical deficiency and national impurity is just as thuggishly
motivated as a common or garden, urban proponent of the
master race.

As the Nazis implemented their racial agenda, Gardiner
became its ready apologist in England. Lauding the German
leadership's 'policy of self-sufficiency and defence based on
the values of yeoman tradition', he claimed that the cause of
the tension between Germany and Britain was 'the irreconcil-
ability of religion and irreligion, the one championing the
values of earth and bread, the other cleaving to the advantages of commerce and usury.' This tension would disappear
if the British returned 'to our own English religion which was
nurtured in the soil of our land until supplanted by alien,
neo-Phoenician ways'.[34] Without personalising his comments, he also attacked Karpeles' position on the Sharp copyright issue.[35]

With mutual friends and colleagues among the hierarchy
of the English Folk Dance and Song Society, Gardiner and
Karpeles were in a position to be aware of the other's views.
And their ideas, philosophy and actions were in complete
opposition to each other. 'We know that what we all want is
magnanimity, manly goals, and that pure religion which is
completely free from the dregs of a stale morality,' Gardiner
wrote in 1933. 'We need what the Germans are in the act of
finding once more: the discipline of togetherness.'[36] To a
Society in the throes of extreme and divisive controversy on
copyright payments and the place of women as dancers and
administrators – in all of which Karpeles figured prominent-
ly – Gardiner's setting manly, freethinking and disciplined
unity as a goal implicitly evoked an opposition that was divisive, woman-oriented and conventional, all the characteris-
tics now attributed to 'Miss Karpeles'. And within the small
group heading the English Folk Dance and Song Society's
organisation, his anti-Semitic comments and views on the
alien nature of 'commerce and usury' would have had a specific reference in Maud Karpeles' race and her links to the
Raphael family's extensive English and continental banking
connections.

As the political crises of the 1930s intensified, conflicts
outside the rarefied world of the Folk Revival were increasingly mirrored by battles within. Writing to Vaughan
Williams about the first performance of his Fourth
Symphony, Karpeles told him, 'Someone said it should have

been called "Europe 1935",' suggesting it conveyed to her 'the feeling of some huge force at work, driving us to fight and struggle, which may eventually shatter us to pieces, and yet we know in our heart of hearts there is something in life which withstands destruction and brings order out of disorder. The secret of it is to be found in music ...' And in November 1936 she used an invitation to speak at the English Folk Dance and Song Society's Silver Jubilee to extend this all-embracing humanitarian interpretation to folk tradition in a comment on dictatorships:

> Cecil Sharp was a real democrat and I think his faith is a very inspiring one in these depressing times ... Dictators and bureaucracies may make the laws of a country, but they have not as yet made the dances or the songs, and however alien and distasteful the actions of a nation may be to us, when we see the people of that nation dancing we recognise them as human beings very much like ourselves.[37]

At the Society's Annual General Meeting in December 1937, Karpeles was successful in introducing the right to an entirely secret ballot for membership of its national executive.[38] Gardiner, however, had already made clear he had little time for democracy, linking it with emasculation and racial impurity. All the European peoples, he wrote in a revealingly worded comment, suffered from an 'impoverishment of their national types', caused on the whole by democracy, which had 'annulled the mystery of power without which men cannot be men, stripped of which they feel deeply humiliated, like a cock despoiled of his plumage.'[39]

Never merely an uninvolved advocate of Fascism as a political ideology, Gardiner took a lead in creating its bases for direct action in England. He was a member of English Mystery, a rural 'school for leadership' organised in 'a sort of cell system designed ultimately to permeate and set the standards for districts, villages and crafts and trades'. In 1936 he also became an officer and propagandist for the extreme right wing, paramilitary English Array, writing regular articles in their *Quarterly Gazette*. In 1938, he published an appreciation of the way in which German leadership in central Europe was spearheading the restoration of national traditions and in

September, attended a camp for English Array officers, encouraging them with a speech which 'showed how hope can be given to a defeated and degenerate nation by sacrifice and singleness of mind working outside the ordinary bureaucratic standards; how the regeneration of Hitler's Germany was made possible beforehand by a few pioneers'.[40] But his vision of using a secret, elite *Männerbund* as a basis for rural power was replicated in each sphere of his influence. 1938 also saw him addressing a meeting of the Morris Ring to propose, 'we are part of an invisible vanguard that is trying to re-establish, not artificially, nor by revolutionary methods, but bit by bit, a more natural way of life'. And he used his own newsletter, *North Sea and Baltic*, to combine his political views and attitudes to traditional dance still more closely:

> ... the Morris and Sword dance are not popular dances: they are essentially selective magic dances which only a peculiarly fitted and trained elite is capable of executing .... It is time that we should begin to restrict and discriminate and to reserve the Morris for a true function in the changing life of our people, and not allow it to be abused by a vogue.[41]

Events were reaching a point of no return. Following a visit to the Baltic in May 1939, Gardiner published a virulent article proposing that 'Riga has the unpleasant air of a cosmopolitan city in which the Jews are the real exploiters of German decline and Lettish incompetence' and 'with the withdrawal of German influence and population it is the Jews who have steadily gained predominance in both Latvia and Lithuania'. The Baltic was 'the natural field of German responsibility,' he wrote, and it would be 'suicidal to oppose Germany in fulfilling it', because 'what is at stake is civilisation and the preservation of the earth from the roving sanddunes of the east'.[42] Gardiner ended his life as Lord Lieutenant of Dorset and a revered speaker at Morris Ring meetings.

Karpeles too had turned her attention to events in Europe. 'With the terrible persecution of the Jews in Germany ... never far from my mind', in May 1938 she began work for an organisation for child refugees, meeting them off the train and finding suitable homes for them. Removed from the

English Folk Dance and Song Society's teaching staff in July
1938, Karpeles made her last defence of the original form of
Sharp's copyright at the Society's annual general meeting
that December and was overwhelmingly defeated. She
remade her working life thereafter almost entirely in her secondary specialisation of song.

Did Gardiner's ideology and activities have any impact on
the career of Maud Karpeles, daughter of a German-Jewish
family and prominent woman administrator? Throughout
the 1930s, Gardiner continued to lecture at Cecil Sharp
House, attend events, contribute to the letters page of the
English Folk Dance and Song Society's magazine and dance
at the annual Morris Ring gathering at Thaxted. Although he
held no office in the English Folk Dance and Song Society, he
was an influential presence and close to the Society's leadership. Douglas Kennedy, who headed both the Society and the
Morris Ring, was a lifelong friend and shared some of his
political associations. In 1941, at a country dance party held
at Gardiner's house, Kennedy became a founder member of
yet another *Männerbund* initiated by Gardiner, 'Kinship in
Husbandry', a 'hidden, unofficial band of friends and accom-
plices' which aimed to combat 'the danger which imperilled
the English tradition ... the bureaucratic or managerial
Welfare State'.[43] Even those who did not remotely accept his
political views have commented on the force of Gardiner's
dominating and persuasive personality:

> Rolf's enthusiasm led him beyond most other
> men. In everything that he did, Rolf was always
> larger than life, a charismatic communicator of
> ideas, becoming a character and a legend in his
> own time. More ordinary men looked on him with
> a certain wonderment.[44]

That Karpeles was barred from holding any position within the English Folk Dance and Song Society's hierarchy in
the 1930s is undeniable. That the Society was at this time also
influenced by a 'charismatic communicator' who was anti-
semitic, antagonistic to women in power and an apologist for
a regime which was simultaneously removing Jews from public life in Germany should not go unremarked.

The outbreak of war in September 1939 saw Karpeles set
up a Refugee Musicians Committee, working with Harriet

Cohen, Hugh Allen, Myra Hess, Ralph Vaughan Williams
and others to provide assistance and jobs for musicians flee-
ing persecution. When her beloved nephew, John Kennedy,
was killed in action in HMS Glow-Worm in April 1940, she
felt determined to contribute more directly to the war effort
and, at the age of 56, spent some months on a production line
making portable radio sets for the Navy. The work was
monotonous and physically demanding, but she records with
characteristic wry humour, it was the choice of background
music which was the most trying aspect her long hours in the
factory. For the rest of the War and into the peace, Karpeles
worked with the Christian Council for Refugees and the Red
Cross. Summing up her character in an obituary for the
International Folk Music Council, Klaus Wachsmann wrote:

> Her sociability and never-boring conversation
> kept her well in touch with events ... and although
> she readily shared her worries, she rarely followed
> advice, but she was a good loser if the Executive
> Board failed to vote in support of her view. She
> had a wonderful sense of humor and a good eye
> for the ridiculous, and life did provide food for
> both occasionally.[45]

In creating a caricature that denies her achievements and in
writing this lively, principled and able woman out of its history, the English Folk Revival has both destroyed and lost much
that is of value.

Notes

I am most grateful to Malcolm Taylor of The Vaughan Williams Memorial
Library, Elaine Bradtke, Chris Sugden, Steve Corrsin, Ken Barr, Martin
Morton, Robin Wiltshire of the National Centre for English Cultural Tradition
and the Staff of Derby Local Studies Library for their kind and unfailing
assistance with sources relating to this work. And to Jim Boyes, Celia Coram
and Julian Putkowski their encouragement and irreplaceable gifts of research
time.

1. Margaret Dean-Smith, 'Dr Maud Karpeles, O.B.E.: 12 November 1885–1 Oct
    1976,' *Folklore*, LXXXVIII:1 (1977), 111.
2. Typescript mss held in Vaughan Williams Memorial Library, English Folk
    Dance and Song Society, AL KARPELES 1366 39.
3. In 1932, the English Folk Dance Society amalgamated with the Folk-Song
    Society to form a conjoint English Folk Dance and Song Society.
4. National Executive Committee [of the English Folk Dance and Song Society],
    The English Folk Dance and Song Society Report Sept 1st to Aug 31st 1933–1934

(London: English Folk Dance and Song Society, 1934), p. 6.

5. Douglas Kennedy, *England's Dances: Folk Dancing To-day and Yesterday* (London: G. Bell & Sons, Ltd, 1949), p. 21.

6. Douglas Kennedy, 'Notes on Recruiting,' *English Dance and Song*, X:6 (1946), p. 74.

7. Douglas Kennedy, 'Obituary: Dr Maud Pauline Karpeles, O.B.E. 1885–1976,' *Folk Music Journal*, III:3 (1977), 292–3 and Fr Kenneth N. J. Loveless, 'Douglas Neil Kennedy, O.B.E.; An Obituary,' *English Dance and Song*, L:1 (April–May 1988), p. 2.

8. Peter Kennedy, 'Everybody's Folk,' *English Dance & Song*, 60:2 (Summer 1998), pp. 24-27.

9. Maud Karpeles, *Cecil Sharp: His Life and Work* (London: Routledge & Kegan Paul Ltd., 1967), p. 120.

10. *Ibid.*, p 103.

11. Quoted in Mike Yates, 'Cecil Sharp in America: Collecting in the Appalachians,' *Musical Traditions Internet Magazine*, MT052, p. 9. Published at www.mustrad.org.uk/articles/shar_txt.htm

12. Karpeles, *Cecil Sharp*, p. 164.

13. Maud Karpeles, 'English Folk Dances: Their Survival and Revival,' *Folk-Lore* XLIII (1932), 141. Paper read at a meeting of the Folk-Lore Society, 21 October 1931.

14. For further detail of Karpeles collecting at this time see *The English Folk Dance Society Report: September 1st 1930, to August 31st 1931* (London: English Folk Dance Society, 1931), p. 16. (All profits from Karpeles' publication of this collection were passed to the English Folk Dance Society); and her papers – 'The Abram Morris Dance,' *Journal of the English Folk Dance and Song Society*, I:1 (Dec. 1932), 55–59; 'Upton-on-Severn Morris Dances,' *Ibid.*, I:2 (Dec. 1933), 101–103; and 'Correspondence: The Lymm (Cheshire) Morris Dance,' *Ibid.*, VI:3 (Dec. 1951), 100–101 which draws on her field notes of 1938.

15. See her comments in Karpeles, 'English Folk Dances: Their Survival and Revival,' p. 141.

16. *Ibid.*

17. Kennedy, 'Obituary: Dr Maud Pauline Karpeles,' p. 293.

18. I am grateful to Steve Corrsin and Ken Barr for their generous assistance in tracing information on the history of the Karpeles and Raphael families and to Martin Morton for his kindness in sending me copies of portions of Evelyn Waley's privately published *International Relations – A brief history of the families from who we are descended with information on the Raphael family*.

19. Maxwell Craven, *Derbeians of Distinction* (Derby: Breedon Books, 1998), p. 166.

20. K. S. Inglis, *Churches and the Working Classes in Victorian England* (London: Routledge & Kegan Paul, 1963), p. 143.

21. Karpeles, *Cecil Sharp*, p. 74 fn.

22. See for example, Mrs [Helen Karpeles] Kennedy, 'Early Days', *E.F.D.S. News* I:7 (May 1924), 172-177; A.H. Fox Strangways, *Cecil Sharp* (Oxford: Oxford University Press, 1933), 78-93 *passim*; Maud Karpeles, 'Past and Present,' *Folk Music Journal* II:2 (1971), 99–101 and Karpeles, *Cecil Sharp*, pp. 74–77.

23. Karpeles, *Cecil Sharp*, p. 116.

24. Roy Palmer, '"Your dancing is simply glorious...": Lavender Jones,' *English Dance & Song* 51:1 (April–May 1989), p. 3.

25. See for example Fred Woods, *Folk Revival: The rediscovery of a national music* (Poole, Dorset: Blandford Press Ltd, 1979), p. 13.

26. Rolf Gardiner, 'Mixed Morris Sides,' *English Dance & Song* I:2 (Nov 1936),

p. 27.

27. Rolf Gardiner, 'The Travelling Morrice and the Cambridge Morris Men,'
    Offprint [1961?] held in The Vaughan Williams Memorial Library, P7145 AS
    14, p. 10.

28. Georgina Boyes, *The Imagined Village: Culture, ideology and the English Folk
    Revival* (Manchester: Manchester University Press 1993), pp 164–179;
    pp. 207–210.

29. Rolf Gardiner, 'Die deutsche Revolution von England gesehen,' in
    Nationalismus von Ausland gesehen (Berlin: 1933) quoted in Richard Griffiths,
    Fellow Travellers of the Right: British Enthusiasts for Nazi Germany 1933–9
    (London: Constable & Co. Ltd, 1980), pp. 74–75.

30. Mike Sutton, 'England, whose England?: Class, gender and identity in the 20th
    century folklore revival,' *Musical Traditions Internet Magazine*, MT083,
    www.mustrad.org.uk/articles/england.htm, p. 7.

31. See Rolf Gardiner, *World Without End: British Politics and the Younger Generation*
    (London: Cobden-Sanderson, 1932), p. 33; 'A Brief Account of the Travelling
    Morrice', *North Sea and Baltic*, New Series, no. 4 (High Summer 1938), 107 and
    England Herself: Ventures in Rural Restoration (London: Faber & Faber Ltd,
    1943), p. 13. For attitudes to *England Herself* within the English Folk Dance and
    Song Society's hierarchy at the time, see Frank Howes' broadly favourable
    review in *Journal of the English Folk Dance and Song Society*, IV:4 (Dec. 1943),
    p. 165.

32. For additional details of Wolfram's career, see Stephen D. Corrsin, *Sword
    Dancing in Europe: A History* (Enfield Lock, Middx: Hisarlik Press for The
    Folklore Society, 1997), pp. 176-182. For examples of his reports, see 'Austria:
    Dr. Richard Wolfram writes,' *Journal of the English Folk Dance and Song Society*
    V:1 (Dec. 1946), 50–51 and V:3 (Dec. 1948), p. 163.

33. Gardiner, 'Mixed Morris Sides,' p. 27.

34. Rolf Gardiner, *Quarterly Gazette of the English Array*, April 1938 quoted in
    Griffiths, *Fellow Travellers of the Right*, p. 146.

35. Rolf Gardiner, Letter on 'traditional forms,' *English Dance and Song* II:2 (1937),
    pp. 30–31.

36. Gardiner, 'Die deutsche Revolution von England gesehen,' p. 18 quoted in
    Griffiths, *Fellow Travellers of the Right*, p. 145.

37. Anon., 'A Jubilee Ball at Cecil Sharp House,' *English Dance & Song* I:3 (Jan.
    1937), p. 35.

38. *The English Folk Dance and Song Society Report Sept 1st, 1937 to August 31st, 1938*
    (London: English Folk Dance and Song Society, 1938), p. 22.

39. Gardiner, 'Die deutsche Revolution von England gesehen', p. 18 quoted in
    Griffiths, *Fellow Travellers of the Right*, p. 145.

40. Rolf Gardiner, *Quarterly Gazette of the English Array*, October 1938 quoted in
    Griffiths, *Fellow Travellers of the Right*, p. 321.

41. Rolf Gardiner, *North Sea and Baltic*, p. 101.

42. Rolf Gardiner, 'Germany and the Baltic States,' *New Pioneer*, May 1939 quoted
    in Griffiths, *Fellow Travellers of the Right*, pp. 326–7.

43. Rolf Gardiner, 'Kinship in Husbandry,' from an unpublished paper, 'European
    Husbandry Meeting' from 'Can Farming Save European Civilisation,' in
    Wessex: Letters from Springhead, Christmas 1950 (Third Series, No. 2) extracts
    reprinted in Andrew Best, ed., *Water Springing from the Ground: An Anthology of
    the Writings of Rolf Gardiner* (Springhead, Dorset: Trustees of the Estate of the
    late H. Rolf Gardiner, 1972), pp. 196–7; see also p. 302. Gardiner's mother was
    of Jewish ancestry and Douglas Kennedy, was married to Helen Karpeles, who

was also Jewish. How Gardiner combined these links with anti-Semitism that went far beyond the casual racism of the day can only be surmised from his early comments praising the effect of the 'filter of German culture' on Jews who then came to England. At the same time, however, he deplored Jews who 'preached hatred against Germany' abroad. Maud Karpeles work for the *Kindertransport* and speaking out against dictatorship may well have brought her into this latter category. See Rolf Gardiner, 'Die deutsche Revolution von England gesehen,' quoted in Griffiths, *Fellow Travellers of the Right*, pp. 74–75. Alternatively, Gardiner and Kennedy, aware of the measures against people of 'mixed race' and marriages between Jews and non-Jews, may simply have been building up a protective case for themselves in the event of a German victory – see Robert Gellately, *Backing Hitler; consent and coercion in Nazi Germany* (Oxford; Oxford University Press, 2001), pp. 122–150.

44. Roy Judge, 'The Evolving Morris: An Introduction,' *The Evolving Morris* (Crewe: The Morris Ring and The Morris Federation, 1991), p. 6.

45. Klaus Wachsmann, 'In Memoriam: Maud Karpeles (1885–1976),' *1976 Yearbook of the International Folk Music Council* (Kingston, Ontario: International Folk Music Council, 1977), p. 10. See also B[runo] N[ettl], 'Editor's Preface,' *1975 Yearbook of the International Folk Music Council* (Kingston, Ontario: International Folk Music Council, 1976), pp. 7–8 for a brief summary of Karpeles significance and activities with the International Folk Music Council.

Further reading

Boyes, Georgina. *The Imagined Village: Culture, ideology and the English Folk Revival*. Manchester: Manchester University Press, 1993.

C[rossley]-H[olland], Peter. 'Editor's Introduction: Ralph Vaughan Williams and Maud Karpeles'. *1972 Yearbook of International Folk Music Council*. N.p.: International Folk Music Council, 1973, pp. 5–8.

Yates, Mike, 'Cecil Sharp in America: Collecting in the Appalachians'. *Musical Traditions Internet Magazine*, MT052. Published at www.mustrad.org.uk/articles/shar_txt.htm

Index